Bayou Roots

LEGACY OF A LOUISIANA FAMILY

ENDORSEMENTS

Congratulations on your book!!! I ordered it the night I got this email! I have now finished it and SOOOO enjoyed it. You have inspired me to get back to work on my "article/sketch" on my paternal Grandfather who went to the Yukon in the Gold Rush. (I don't have anywhere near the source material that you did though.)

I am fascinated by the use of Creative Nonfiction; I did not know that genre and my, did it work so well for this book. It is so very readable on a number of levels – history, genealogy, geography, family "philosophy" and heritage. By reading your Acknowledgments, I see that your writers' network was a great help; what a blessing. This book is an absolutely wonderful gift to your family; so special.

Thank you for letting me know of its publication. Now do you feel as if you have nothing to do (ha! I bet), have birthed another child, lost 100 pounds or some such??!! Hope Spring is good in your area.

All the best – and again, congratulations!

—**Elaine Bolton**, Retired Executive Director of
Macon Heritage, Macon, Georgia

You did a great job. It was interesting throughout, interesting enough to hold my attention even when my eyes tired. I actually (and quite seriously) see this as a best seller, especially among the genealogy crowd. I don't have to be you or your family to enjoy it.

—**Lynn Moffett**, author of
Blood, Flesh and Flame; *Dark Secret, Silent Promise*;
and *An Honorable Anger*

Bayou Roots
LEGACY OF A LOUISIANA FAMILY

April Adamson Holthaus

LEGACY
PRESS

PAGOSA SPRINGS, CO

Cover & Interior Design: Derinda Babcock

PUBLISHED BY: Legacy Press, 182 Driftwood Drive, Pagosa Springs, CO 81147

Library Cataloging Data
Name: Holthaus, April Adamson (April Adamson Holthaus)
Bayou Roots/ April Adamson Holthaus
190 p. 23cm x 15cm (9in x 6 in.)
Description: Legacy Press | POD paperback edition | Legacy Press 2018.
Identifiers: ISBN-978-0-692-04976-1|(POD)Key Words: Women—Non-fiction.
2. Louisiana history—Non-fiction. 3. Louisiana genealogy—Non-fiction. 4.
Memoir—1818—2000

DEDICATION

Rowena Elaine LaCoste Adamson
My mother —The writer, linguist, poet
• •

Carolyn Elaine Smith Riedberger Springer
Andrea Leigh LaCoste Holthaus Sprague
My two daughters
• •

Kailey Marie Smith Wiggers
Rebekah Ruth Riedberger
Sydney Taylor Smith Quiller
Kassidy Jo Smith Brueckner
LeighAnna & Lydia
My six granddaughters
• •

Ivy Lucille Wiggers
Eryn Marie Wiggers
Eden Yvette Koenig
My three great-granddaughters
• •

Katherine LaCoste Adamson Bowers
Ruth Beatriz Adamson Yowell
Eleanor Rowena Adamson Keisman
My nieces

TABLE OF CONTENTS

FOREWARD

Dear Reader,

I would like to thank my sister, April, for making the extraordinary effort to create this book. She and I speculated and wondered for at least fifty years about the stories we were told by our mother and grandmother. We wanted to know more about the people and events they described. By searching through the letters saved by our grandmother Pennock, we were able to confirm and fill out the stories that we only knew in part.

April also searched in courthouses, libraries, on websites, and contacted distant relatives to gain additional information. I am grateful to her for bringing an appreciation and richness to my understanding of our family history that I would have never otherwise known.

Linda Adamson

our Stretch
... 73 · pitalidie   founded 1893   New Orleans, L

ACKNOWLEDGMENTS

My heartfelt thanks to many family and friends, who encouraged me and showed interest to make this book possible.

My sister, LINDA ADAMSON, was the first to read and sort the many letters written decades ago by our mother and grandmothers. This book is based on those letters. She read countless reworked pages of copy and gave helpful suggestions when her memory of events was better than mine. She's been my "heart" cheerleader.

JANE HALL, our consummate family genealogist helped check details of family history. She kept me on track with her suggestions. Her husband Greg and I share our great-grandmother, Almira.

A dear friend, BARBARA ROWZEE, the yack-in-your-ear friend, read, reread, edited and listened to each chapter. As a Louisianan, her background understands the time and place of *Bayou Roots*.

Members of the Wolf Creek Christian Writers Network have given insightful feedback and critique. JAN DAVIS, LINDA FARMER HARRIS, PAM HAYES, CAROLYN JOHNSON, LYNN MOFFETT, BETTY SLADE, RICHARD GAMMILL, GREG HEID, BETH JOYCE, CHARLES WENZEL and KATHY ZILLHAVER.

Through this group I met DERINDA BABCOCK, an amazing designer who created this amazingly perfect cover and produced the format for pre-publishing. Her expertise gave me confidence to experience this new journey.

Research librarians at the Houma Library, the Houma Court House and the New Orleans City Library, went out of their way to help me find the documents I needed.

This quote from, Our Story McCalla to McCauley, by Samuel L. McCauley acknowledges the many benefits of knowing your family history. "*...despite any of their shortcomings or frailties, we nevertheless stand upon their shoulders to become whatever we are today. We see how one person's life can affect the world around them and how they helped create the forces that shaped how we were raised and have a framework with which to build our own futures and lives.*"

I hope our family and my readers will realize their decisions and life events can influence future generations.

Note: *Letters are quoted. Misspellings or grammar errors were not corrected.*

Treasures Discovered

CHAPTER ONE

THE DISCOVERY

Rowena Elaine Adamson, our mother, was buried on a cool November day in 2012. Her ashes, in the delicate Grieving Angel container, waited under the graveside canopy. She'd requested her final resting place be with her mother and grandparents at Lake Lawn Metairie Cemetery in New Orleans.

My sister Linda put her arm around my shoulder and whispered, "We did what she asked."

The large granite cross on the family plot sparkled in the sun. It directed our attention to the carving —H.L. Nick, for most us there our great, or great-great grandfather.

For a New Orleans funeral, culture proscribes what's called a "second line band," complete with brass instruments and silly bobbing umbrellas. Music had been a very important part of Mother's life and we wanted it to be part of her service, but how? Fortunately, a talented violin student offered to play at the graveside. The lovely strains of the aria, "O Mio Bambino Caro," one of mom's favorite, wafted softly over the area as we waited to begin.

Father John, his white cassock set off by a closely trimmed white beard and shock of white hair, officiated the Episcopal service, his comforting demeanor soothed our final goodbyes. He closed with an uplifting poem on grief Mother had written years ago.

Linda rose to speak. "Mother was attracted to a life of music, mainly voice which she studied in college. After graduation, she continued lessons in France for the summer and was invited to continue lessons with a small opera company in Paris. Hitler's plans changed hers. The dream was left behind. Her mother did not support her wish to have a career in music. Academic study was something she felt better suited her daughter's future employment."

My brother Marque spoke for our family too as he reminded us of many aspects of Mom's life that were important to him. "She definitely made sure we knew she loved us. The passion of her life's work, teaching foreigners to speak English, showed her fire for an area of education benefiting others."

A large spray of Hawaiian blossoms she loved rested above her grandfather's name. They also spoke of our father buried in Hawaii. Other guests laid bouquets on the grassy plot near the cross.

At that solemn moment, I became aware six of our ancestors were buried here, each part of our New Orleans heritage. They are our roots in the soil and bayous of Louisiana. Linda was right, *"with mother, everybody was here."*

***

After the graveside service, reservations awaited fifteen of us at Commanders Palace, an historic New Orleans eatery. Linda, our two brothers, Marque and Eric, many of our children, and me, April Holthaus, shared memories of previous New Orleans visits and meals enjoyed at "The Palace."

Linda leaned in so everyone could hear. "I remember Grammy Rowena telling me about her unforgettable sixth birthday at this restaurant in 1899, just she and her father came."

"I came here with Mom and Grammy a few times," Eric, (our wine connoisseur brother), spoke up. I ordered their best champagne. This wonderful place was always their first choice."

As our meal ended I clinked my glass a few times. "Thanks everyone for coming from around the country to honor Mother. Some of us called her Mom, or Grammy or, a few thought of her as Elaine. At the end of a long life, her ashes are next to her mother and grandparents. She almost made it to her ninety-fifth birthday, next week - November 15. This evening is special as we all celebrate her life together. It's also an opportunity to learn more about our family history in New Orleans and Louisiana while we're here."

Everyone raised a glass. "To Mom. Grammy. God be with you. Happy Birthday."

***

After dinner my niece, Ruth, asked me, "Aunt April, I'm curious. Grammy was the last one from here. Will we ever come here again?"

"Who can ever tell what the future holds, Ruth. There are still things to discover about our family that could lead in new directions. I'll be back for sure and let you know."

***

The next day familiar sights and aromas of the French Quarter surrounded my sister and me as we strolled its narrow streets. "Linda, I remembered our childhood vacations here at Mardi Gras. This city gave me icky feelings. Must have been voodoo in the air."

"Well, I concentrated on catching beads and cups from the floats. I wasn't scared. It was just fun."

"That's 'cause you were younger and didn't know better."

On Royal Street we paused to photograph intricate Spanish lace balconies. Our pace quickened as the scent of warm beignets drew us toward Jackson Square. Restaurants we passed along the buckled sidewalks tempted us with their signs for fresh oysters or po'boy sandwiches.

"Let's talk at the French Market," Linda suggested.

"Great. It's not a visit to New Orleans until we've tasted chicory coffee with a side of those sugared beignets."

We sat overlooking Jackson Square and the passing tourists. "April, my interest in our family history is heightened by what we've seen today, just being here. What did you find in the old stuff in the basement when you came here to help Mom move to Virginia? You and I had only a brief time to open a few of those letters together."

"Well, the letters and my genealogy research can verify our ancestors have lived in Louisiana for about 213 years. Before 1800, the Knight family from Pennsylvania settled near Opelousas Post. To obtain land they swore allegiance to the King of Spain."

"Generations after were either born in the city or found their way from France and Germany. I'll still be looking for more answers hidden in those boxes."

"Too bad I live so far away in Hawaii," Linda sighed. "Keep me posted."

***

In 1985 Mom moved from Washington, DC, to New Orleans to care for her mother, our Grammy Rowena. When she passed, in early 1993, Mom inherited the home on Nashville Avenue. It was full of years of possessions.

In February 2001, I went to New Orleans to move Mom near our brother Eric in Virginia. Health concerns demanded she live closer to family. Moving those *treasurers* became my nightmare. My only relief from clearing and packing the house was daily phone calls to Linda to gripe and complain.

"Linda, there's at least 50 years worth of stuff to touch and sort through. And this house has been flooded many times in this below-sea-level city. Water damage. Oh, my gosh." I took a breath. "The decisions are endless. Mom is so angry with me. She thinks the disruption to her life, is me taking away her freedom. I want to scream—or run and hide. I don't want to hurt her, but we decided this has to be done, didn't we?"

Why is this was my responsibility? Why did I take this on by myself?

"I'm truly sorry you're doing this alone. If I could, I'd be there. So call me any time for emotional backup, OK?

***

Linda and I had grown increasingly aware of changes in Mom. Conversations with her indicated vagueness in thinking and hesitancy to reveal her decisions. I found checks for a large amount of money written to a stranger. A repairman had over charged her for some repairs to her roof. These items were only the beginning of her obvious financial confusion.

***

On my next call, I gave Linda more details. "This house is overflowing with decades of used books, old magazines, and newspapers—stacked everywhere. There are seven ironing boards placed over the furniture. She uses them as tables with files on top. In the basement block and board shelves are loaded with wrinkled books and boxes. The odor of mold lingers, and dead bugs are underneath everything I move."

The city's floods and semi-tropical climate damaged many of her belongings. But she couldn't tell. Unceremoniously I hauled piles of them to the curb. Mom would agree, then, sneak out to retrieve things when I wasn't looking.

One miserable, hot, sticky afternoon Mom sarcastically asked, again, "Why do you throw my things out? I'm not onboard with all this." I did not answer, for the 100th time.

I ignored her and reached to remove a flimsy box from the highest shelf. One and two-cent stamps fell from its loose bottom. Inside I discovered hundreds of envelopes and letters. Unable to contain my excitement, I quickly gave Mom some to read and ran upstairs to call Linda.

"You won't believe what I've found," I shouted. "Family names, addresses, old postal dates—all on moldy envelopes—letters and photographs inside. Eureka! Family gold!"

"Sounds like you hit the mega jack pot. Don't stop now, tell me more."

"I opened four more boxes. Grammy must have saved this stuff for 80 years, at least. I'm touching real family treasures; thoughts of people Mom and Grammy told us about. These are what we'd hoped to find to verify their stories."

Priceless old photographs slid out of dried glue envelopes. I estimated about 400 letters; moldy-but-precious, and still readable. Written in pencil or green or blue ink. I was as excited as I'd ever been on Christmas morning. I wanted to dive in and open them all, right then.

Carefully shifting through the top layer of one box, I saw a torn piece of paper with writing on it stuck to the outside of an envelope. In tiny script, my great, great grandmother, Fannie, had written her parent's names, William and Frances Ann Stringer Knight. She connected them with a small thin line to the word Houma. I'd found another generation. I knew for sure our family roots were planted in Louisiana.

***

Years later, after a second move, Mom's stuff was put in storage near my home. Care for her became the priority.

When Linda came to visit Mom and me in Colorado it was time to read some of those letters together.

We settled on my office floor: open boxes all around us. We separated the fragile pages, carefully shook out dry black mold and sorted each by year and writer.

Confessions and forgotten dreams unfolded of people we barely knew. "Listen to this," Linda gasped. "Grammy's divorce from Joe in

1942 wasn't like she'd led us to believe. They both filed but she let him be the bad guy."

"I know divorces has two sides. I sensed from her other letters she'd been deeply hurt, even if she was expecting it. This was her second one. Another woman is hard to fight."

***

I searched another box and my hand touched tissue paper wrapped around an embossed-cover memory album and read its first page.

"Linda, here's a beautiful poem dedicated to Fannie by her mother, Frances Ann. *It's dated 1859.*"

The date took a moment to sink in. "This was written before the Civil War! It's also the year *before* Gramma Fannie Knight married Frank Brown." Near the back I saw a signature: *Sidney L. Farmer, New Orleans, 1865.* "Our great, great grandfather signed this. He was Fannie's second husband, our great grandmother Almira's father."

These signatures excited me more than anything we'd found. Not only were we reading their thoughts but also our hands were touching what their hands had written. A direct link to our family's past.

***

Linda sat back and took it all in. "We've been given these precious gifts and it's up to us to make sense of our discovery. You and I are the middle generation between our ancestors, our children and your ten great grandchildren."

I agreed. "Musty unidentified objects may not mean much to future generations without explanations. We have our work cut out for us."

"I'm surprised how connected I feel to people I've never met."

"You and I at least know who they are."

"I'm glad I love genealogy and can put each person in their correct family line."

"Our ancestor's lives have to be told otherwise they'll be lost. It's fortunate Grammy labeled some of the personal things."

"Guess we leave it there for now. Thanks for your help. It's been exciting."

"My flight leaves tomorrow morning. Wish I could stay longer to visit Mom and do more."

***

Sometime later I opened a letter dated August 1939. Grammy had sent it from New York to her sister, Ella in New Orleans. She'd written a blow-by-blow description of the trauma she and Elaine (our mother) experienced escaping from Paris. They'd sailed on the *Isle de France*, the last ship to cross the Atlantic as Hitler made his way into France that September. My hands shook when I thought of our tenuous link to life.

Other letters revealed more details of the thoughts of five women of different eras yet connected to us by family and blood. Their trials, successes and courage are our legacy.

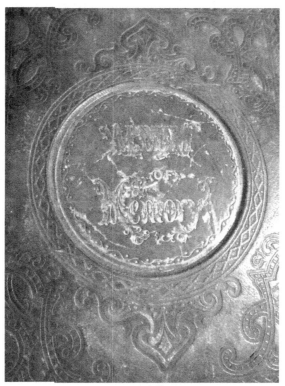

Memory Album

FRANCES ANN
1818-1869

FRANCES ANN STRINGER KNIGHT BELL

FAMILY CHART

Frances Ann Stringer—Knight, Bell—b. 1818—d. July 1869
> (1) William Knight—b. 1817—d. Oct 8, 1851
> m. January 14, 1837

> Children:

>>   Theodora (Dora) Christine—b. 1838—d. 1922
>>   Corinne Elizabeth—b. 1840—d. 1844
>>   **Frances Fredericka (Fannie)—b. 1843—d. 1920**
>>   Reuben—b. 1846—d. 1879
>>   William—b. 1849—d. 1864

> (2) James Madison Bell—b. 1826—d. 1862/3
> m. March 14, 1853

CHAPTER TWO

*W*hen I saw her name for the first time, I began a fascinating journey with Frances Ann, my third great-grandmother. Her name was one connected by the small line to the word Houma on a torn scrap of paper. Houma had not been a place, nor Frances Ann a person, mentioned in any family discussions. This elusive clue had broken through a brick wall of frustration in my search for our southern Louisiana roots. Within six months of this discovery I booked a trip to Houma, Louisiana.

***

My search in Houma began at the imposing stone 19th century Terrebonne Parish Courthouse. A knowledgeable assistant directed me to a large land-record book. In it I found a William Knight, his wife Frances Ann and their four children, Theodora, Frances, Reuben and William. They were residents of the parish from 1841 to 1854 on a sugarcane plantation located on Bayou Black.

Other records and documents of court proceedings connected me to Frances Ann Stringer Knight and her daughter, Frances Fredericka Knight, my second great- grandmother. A new line was established to her daughter, Almira Lee Anna Farmer, my great grandmother. Then to her daughter Rowena Corinne Nick, my grandmother and her daughter, Rowena Elaine LaCoste, my mother.

Renewed interest in this line of our family, combined with history of the 1800 and 1900's, helped to blend historical facts and the genre of Creative Nonfiction, to complete this family legacy.

***

A woman of another century shared my DNA and connected me to 200 years of Louisiana history.

January 19, 1852

*F*rances Ann took her pencil, smoothed a sheet of paper on the small candlelit table and wrote: My Memories

"On nineteenth day of January 1837, I became Mrs. William Knight. It was fifteen years ago today we traveled to Mobile, Alabama to marry at the courthouse. Not a long journey from our homes in New Orleans but the place our new adventures began together.

This adventure ended three months ago on October 8, 1851. My dear husband, William, died that day. His illness began quickly and two house calls by the doctor could not reverse his condition. I prayed fervently for his recovery, leaving the outcome to our Creator, but now I grieve my painful loss and broken heart. Facing a future with the heavy burden of widowhood and a life without William is daunting.

This entanglement of grief flows from my fingers as I commit confusing thoughts to paper. Seeing my pain written down begins to separate it from weakened emotions I cannot abide if I wish to persevere.

***

I have such sweet memories of how William and I met. That day began when I asked permission to accompany our houseboy Thomas to market to buy supplies for mother. New Orleans bustled with morning commerce as he and I stepped out early to avoid the oppressive heat of that summer day of 1836. Though chaperoned, this was my one opportunity to be "alone," even for a short while. It was not *comme it faut* (as it was done) for a young lady like myself to be seen on the street, but I felt safe with Thomas.

Father heard us leaving and warned from the parlor, "Avoid Royal Street. I don't want either of you accosted." My father, G.R. Stringer, a busy exchange slave broker and notary, had his office on the corner of Charters and Conti in the Quarter. His door opened to the sidewalk and conversations for any number of activities were easy to hear as people shared news in the street.

"Yes father," I answered, an obedient daughter, "we'll go straight there and home again. We have to hurry before the Market closes at ten o'clock."

We went along a familiar route down Charters to the corner of Decatur Street and then to the Market. Thomas knew my brother Jackson, a clerk at Mechanics and Traders Bank, was close enough to come to our aid if we had trouble with pirates, or anything else.

***

A hand brushed mine as I reached for a string of garlic at the market.
"Oh, pardon me miss," he said.

I remember I blushed and drew back.

"May I assist you to find fresh oysters or other items today? I buy each day for Dudley and Knight Grocers, my place of employment on Tchoupitoulas. My name is William Knight."

That was nice of him, but we hadn't been properly introduced.

"Thank you, Mr. Knight. Our family enjoys oysters. And okra, oh, and corn too, especially in Mama's special holiday stuffing."

Did I say too much? In spite of my shyness our short conversation excited me.

***

I volunteered often to go to market with Thomas, where I would see William. Within a few months of our meeting, he asked father for permission to court me and I eagerly agreed. After a proper year we discussed marriage, to which father again gave his permission.

I was going to be married. There were so many things to think about and prepare for. I would need a new dress. Where and when would we marry? Would I be a kind and caring wife to William?

Because the Financial Panic of 1837 hurt father's business, he felt our wedding should not be elaborate. We decided to travel to the Mobile Alabama Courthouse, where our ceremony was recorded on January 19, 1837. A later announcement in the *New Orleans Commercial Bulletin*, informed our friends and family of the details of our wedding.

I don't remember why a place in New Orleans wasn't chosen.

William was established in his business in the City. Our home reflected the values of family, home and faith. My nearby parents and brother enjoyed close family times with our two daughters, Dora and Corinne, born during those first four years.

***

William's grocery business provided for us during the long financial depression. People had to eat. Often we discussed if New Orleans was the best place to raise our children. I'd spent my childhood in the Uptown Carrollton area, but our ongoing distress focused on the horrible lack of sanitation in the city. A torrent of new immigrants in the early 1840's compounded these problems. They and the rainstorms that flooded this below sea-level city, caused epidemics of diphtheria, typhoid, malaria, and always, yellow fever. Residents were frightened and chose to find ways to escape to the country, especially in the hot summer months.

***

William wrote to his younger brother Michael in Bayou Black.

Could you recommend a place near you for our family to stay this summer? Frances Ann and I want to avoid these frightening diseases and what is happening here in the City. William

Instead, Michael's answer encouraged us to obtain land in Houma near Bayou Black. William and I agreed it would be healthful for the girls and perhaps more lucrative for our future. William had done well in the grocery business, but I wondered if he knew how to run a plantation.

We moved to Houma in 1841.

Before we left New Orleans, William's older brother, Joseph bequeathed three slaves to me. The legal documents we signed on February 21, 1840, indicated his *"affection for his sister-in-law, Frances Ann Stringer."* I took possession of Lila, Craig, and Patience, with her two young children, George and Levet. . . . *"to be hers and her heirs forever hereby abrogating the law... and valued at the sum of two thousand nine hundred dollars."*

***

Bayou Black

My heart was heavy as we left New Orleans and everything I'd known in my twenty-two years. I watched my family until I could not see them anymore. As we started out I knew I needed to change my focus and whole-heartedly welcome our new adventure. William was excited and mentioned he looked forward to proving himself.

Bayou Black from the bridge

Our slaves loaded the wagon for the 58-mile trip. The journey took us along the river and bayous—near alligators and snakes—that required everyone to be prepared should dire situations occur. It took most of two days to reach Bayou Black, a place we had never seen.

***

In preparation William read, *DeBow's Review*, a popular agriculture and commercial journal with articles encouraging settlement in the South. It calmed my fears with a particular article on this very area, *"Oak Grove on Bayou Black."*

As a city girl, I'd envisioned a swamp-infested backwoods. The article referred to Bayou Black as containing *more tillable land than in any other parish*. It stated the bayou's population was *thickly inhabited with the refinements and blessing of society*. Fine dwellings, with *yards and gardens arranged with taste and comeliness*. It continued, many planters on these various bayous *add to society the benefit of intelligence with pleasant conversation*. We later saw great improvements in the parish with respect to schools and churches. Recently the parish priest had documented forty houses in the parish seat of Houma.

In contrast to New Orleans, we found bountiful resources nearby: ducks, turkeys, deer, geese, pheasants, quails and all the fish we could eat. We grow almost everything else we need except a little flour, powder and salt. William found a bonanza of muskrat, raccoon, otter, rabbit, opossums and mink in these vast marshes. Fortunately, hunters had reduced other wildlife like bobcats, leopards, wolves and cougars.

In Houma a large brick schoolhouse, and Catholic and Methodist churches, were newly built. An older Methodist church on Bayou Black allowed even our slaves to participate in religious services. The folks on Bayou Black warmly welcomed us into their predominantly French plantation society. It was a relief to my weak spirit to find a former wilderness flourishing with sugar production and livestock.

Court record described William's property as: "Arpents on the left bank of Bayou Black together with all the sugar—and all the improvements thereon...appraised together at $12,000." [in 2016 value $358,313.]

***

July 1843

Dear Mother,

I've found Bayou Black society not a backwoods situation. I consider myself the wife of an upcoming sugar planter. When we do travel into the village of Houma there are goods and services available from the growing wealth here. Although far from being a creature of leisure, as a plantation mistress there are days when quite a bit of that black earth is on my hands too. Working alongside a slave in our garden allows me to experience the progress of our "wealth" and food. I am training my girl Lila for household duties which includes the kitchen garden.

You'll be pleased to know activities I enjoy in the community include quilting parties. I use scraps from items Lila makes for us. Personally I'm in need of fashionable attire only when I visit socially on nearby plantations.

I know you are anticipating an announcement that I am with child. Yes, this new one I carry is much desired. In the spring maybe it will be a boy for William. My focus for my little ones is their safety, welfare, and schooling. I feel fulfilled as a wife, mother and mistress of our expanding family and plantation.

My religious duties please me as I instill the disciplines of piety in my children, as you taught me Mother. I participate in a ladies study of the Bible, teach a children's Sunday class occasionally, and help raise funds with my jams or sugar candies.

As I enjoy the breezes this evening, hearing the children at play, I have sad thoughts of our precious little Corinne who died last year. A mother's heart never recovers nor forgets one she's lost. Our dear Dora comforts me, as she is a sweet older sister to our baby Fannie. We are well and pray you, Father and brother are also.

Your loving daughter, Frances Ann

***

Again I write on a quiet Sunday afternoon and have moments to reflect about our lives here. How thankful I am we are well settled. The fields in our section of Bayou Black stretch as far as the eye can see, at least until the next marsh. Sugar cane grows tall in this good black earth. The loose green cane tops wave in a breeze from the Gulf. Our field slaves will be working there again tomorrow until sunset. Long, hard days are required to produce sugar. William informed me he'd recently bought more land and farm implements. He's learning the plantation business is never ending with three harvests a year.

The fields are fully planted as I look south from the comfortable veranda encircling our home. Here, life's cycles—plantings and harvests— are not only constant reminders of our Creator, but give life a peaceful rhythm. Yes, I can rest a while.

***

Spring, 1849

Living out of a city allowed us to fashion our home in a traditional Southern style. Broad overhanging eaves bring such relief from the intense, nearly year-round, Louisiana heat and humidity. This design anticipates welcome flow-through Gulf breezes to cool our home. Generously scaled tall ceilings and our Southern full-height windows with wooden shutters give a pleasing look to the wrap-around veranda. Our evening's repose, in large rocking chairs, is a perfect end to a long, busy day.

***

From here I also glance down the row of slave cabins William had built. Their one room floors are planked, walls whitewashed, and a small porch out front allows for sittin' after work. There are buildings for animals, another for farming equipment and one for cooking. The sugar shed was built furthest away for safety as fires burn there day and night.

Sugar making is our business. I've observed the ponderous process. The slaves push rough stalks into a crusher to release sweet flowing juice. A pipe carries it to a large cauldron balanced on bricks over a wood fire, heated, they say, to over 200 degrees. The mixture is continuously stirred and skimmed. I've tended many a burnt slave, grown tired or careless on that duty.

Sugar cauldron

With two to three plantings of cane a year, sugar is a valuable crop. The hogsheads are filled with 63 gallons for export to New Orleans by boat. William says we can anticipate a good profit each year.

***

Taking time to write in my journal has proved beneficial. Even these brief notes give me a sense of my life's pace. In the 1850 Census our plantation and sugar business were valued at $14,000. Our plantation was also mentioned in other settlement information as being one of the 110 large plantations in the area. It's evident there's a future for us here.

William just showed me a paper he'd signed to purchase additional equipment. It was also signed by Mr. James M. Bell. It read:

January 1851, "...to be paid $450 on the first day of March 1863, .. .for one sugar mill, kettles, grates, bricks, and coolers ... situated at the mouth of Bayou Black with eight per cent interest from maturity until paid. (Signed) —W. Knight, James M. Bell."

***

I'm remembering what our plans were for our life here. Help me write this, dear Lord. My tears fall without stopping. Our—my dream is gone. William is dead.

***

December, two months later—Christmas 1851

I've recently met with Mr. Goode, the administrator William placed over his affairs. He showed me William's extensive debts, totaling over $5000. William had not faithfully discharged many of his responsibilities. I imagine he thought he would eventually. Now I find woven into my deep personal loss, worries over the financial situation of the plantation.

I am shocked. The list includes multiple mortgages on our land, ten personal loans, three years unpaid back taxes, sheriff's fees, and administrator's fees. The final entries are his last two doctor's visits of $47.60 and $64.03. *Oh, Father what to do? It's a final blow to pay the $28.32 for his coffin.*

I questioned Mr. Goode as to how these debts would be paid and what would happen to my children and me. I'm thankful some of my responsibilities these past ten years strengthened me for tasks I now must shoulder alone. As a wife, I deferred all things monetary or concerning business to my husband. Now I must rely on others I fear to trust.

Since Mother passed in 1847 and Father two years later, I am an orphan. I find no one to lift these weights from my heart and shoulders.

Mr. Goode reminded me politely of a law the State of Tennessee recently passed in 1849 that states, *"married women lack independent souls and thus should not be allowed to own property."*

I read the rest of it almost without comprehending for its insolence. *"Even where statutes appeared to establish some measure of rights for a married woman, courts interpreted the statutes to her disadvantage ..."*

William did not leave a will to give directions for our care. I fear he's left our future to unknown chances. Recently though, in 1850, laws as to women's inheritance are changing. I am informed I could inherit for my children after being appointed their legal guardian. That is my next step.

***

The Christmas service this week focused my thoughts on the Lord's promise, "to always be with me." Otherwise, with our grief so fresh, the holiday has not been pleasing. The winter view of empty fields is bleak, like my spirit.

I try to assess my situation as a young widow. I am 33 years old, with four young children, 11, 8, 6, and 4. I struggle to comprehend a man's world of finance. Mr. Goode controls when and where we receive financial resources according to the law. Where do I go for help?

Frances, be strong, there is much for me to learn. These ponderous facts seem a sterile account of the multiple events and depth of the surrounding difficulties and future I dread to face.

***

February 1852

Since William's death in October, I've waited in limbo to be granted guardianship of and given funds to care for my children. Thankfully neighbors have shared their bounty. Finally, I am appointed legal Tutrix (guardian) of William's heirs, my own minor children. I pray this is a permanent solution for us. I was informed that *all inventory should remain unmoved until the sugar crop is harvested in June 1852. Then the debts of the estate would be paid. The sale of the home at a future time.*

Court records insist on an inventory of my property. But any monies to relieve our struggle are still months away. I keep this journal of my days and the events surrounding me to record our search for provisions. This news gives me hope that the children and I can remain in the

Movable Property:
2-doz chairs, $6 ea.
2-rocking chairs, $2.50 ea.
1-wash stand and bowl, $4
2-beds/
   bedsteads-complete, $30
1-dressing glass, $6
board, $8
1-bookcase, $10
couches and mattress, $6
3-tables and sofa, $12
1-lot glassware
crockeryware, $15
1-lot kitchen utensils, $10
a riding saddle and bridle, $30
a double-barrel shotgun, $5
5-spades and 3 shovels, $3.50
8-hoes and 1 grabbing iron, $1
3-doz 2-ft edgers, $4
1 broad ax and hatchet, $2
6-axes, $3
5-ploughs, $10
1-harrow, #3
1-set Cooper tools, $6
30-barrels of corn, $15
1 large cart, $35
2 cart-2 pair cartwheels, $36
2 log chains, $3
2 cross-cut saws and 1 chop saw, $10
1-lot of blacksmith tools and iron, $20
TOTAL: $354.50
Land and Household:
$12,000
TOTAL Property: $18,612

comfort of our home. They are suffering the loss of their father deeply, especially William, just 5 years old now.

A month after harvest on the 26th of July, I was again confirmed *natural Tutrix (guardian) of my minor children.* There is a certain kindness in these delays the court is allowing. Time to formulate a plan of action. But I see no relief about the debts.

***

An inventory of my household was taken after the June harvest but did not result in any sales or benefit of funds. The sugar that did sell after June harvest was not enough to clear debts or provide funds we needed.

***

The court now insists our property be sold. It's been less than a full year since William's death. I've searched to find new living arrangements for the children and myself as I've grieved our loss and worried about our future. There are things to be grateful for but also to remain patient in this process. I've even thought about a possible future on Bayou Black by seeking advice from my brother-in-law, Michael.

My life is changing in so many ways. Another inventory has given the court control of our possessions. Soon the sale of our slaves will be top priority to pay William's debts. They are my most valuable assets but it's difficult for me to see them sold and not know if they will be treated well. We've been together over fourteen years in a relationship difficult to define. But I do care they are treated well.

The back and forth in the confusion of this sale requires that our slaves are needed to work the fields to produce a crop that can be sold to pay our debts. But they also need to be sold to pay the debt.

Slaves were listed as:
David, 52 years, $500
Abram, 32 years, $900
Jack, 23, years, $500
Clara, 50 years, $100
Seintha, 24 years with infant, Mary Elizabeth, $900
Emelia, 21 years with infant, Henry, $700
Delpha, 31 years, three children, Henrietta, 6 years, Leonidas, 4 years, Martha, 8 months, $1000
Sally Anne, 12 years, $400
Clara, 15 years, $450
Total Value of Slaves: $5,450

***

A Strange Future—1853

James Madison Bell, William's friend and business partner proposed marriage. I felt he was the best solution to stave off horrible future consequences to my children and myself. We married on March 14. Unfortunately, our marriage dream affected the law regarding William's succession.

***

Court records stated, " ... *subsequent in the early part of 1853 she intermarried with her present husband, James M. Bell, but being ignorant of the law and of her duty under it, she failed to call a (Knight) family meeting previous to her marriage and thereby is deprived of the Tutrix (guardian) of her children.*"

I unknowingly took a step that would strip me of the guardianship of my children and the resources due to them. I innocently chose security and a stable partner to help me through the morass of a man's legal world. *Now what am I to do?*

***

December 28, 1853

There's another court order for a third inventory of my property, if I still even own it. It's unbelievable they would desecrate the Christmas season this way. This last hearing ordered the slaves, mules, horses, and miscellaneous property sold at public auction by the first Monday of February 1854. William's remaining debts would potentially be cleared up, funds for the children's welfare would be provided and my legal battles with William's family would end.

But to regain guardianship of my children the court required me to post a bond. I was frantic. James and I did not have that kind of money. Michael, William's younger brother, was made guardian of my children, controlled their inheritance and assumed custody. He did not offer to pay the bond. If he is only obeying the law, then I am confused. All I can imagine is a "legal right of succession" was more important than William's children. I assumed him cruel. What could I have done so wrong? I unknowingly remarried without their consent? In the meantime James and I are frustrated that the children must remain with Michael until I am again declared their legal guardian, not even named their mother, The situation is breaking my heart. I have James beside

There is no evidence that the children lived with her or were given to their Uncle Michael. But the definition of guardianship usually involved a child living with a guardian. "Guardians have physical custody, and the child's parent does not. However, biological parents maintain their parental rights, even when they don't have physical custody." www.legalzoom.com

21

me, but my children have lost both their father and now the comfort of their mother.

***

I petitioned many times for the required Knight family meetings to take place and rule on my guardianship. Why this is moving so slowly has no answer. Justice, takes its own time I fear. I am without recourse with the court and William left no written instructions for our care. Making final papers may not have occurred to a man like William, only 34 years old.

It's two years since his death. I feel myself weak against rules that don't answer my questions. When will this legal frustration end? The sugar sales have been stretched out for two years without enough to pay the debts.

***

Moving—1854

James and I took a long last look at my home on Bayou Black. Watching my children cared for by others, as well as fearing for my own emotional stability, we felt we must separate from here.

It was my home for thirteen years. The last three in an uncomfortable unresolved legal situation with the Knight family. I'd been unrelenting in my requests for legal action to be renamed Tutrix (guardian) of my children. It broke my heart to leave them now.

James and I moved to St. Charles Parish, a day away. After two more long years, we were given reason to hope. We received word of and responded by letter to a new Knight family meeting held at the Terrebonne Court House. It was held without us. We waited for the outcome and a positive answer to our prayers.

In 1856, finally the documents decreed, *"Mrs. Frances Ann Bell be and is hereby appointed to retain in the tutorship of her minor children and entitled to receive the amount coming to her minor children."* Also, *"the right of keeping the Negro, Daisy for the mutual interest of herself and her minors."*

We rejoiced over the $4,000 that came with those orders. In August an additional amount of $1,698.32 was sent. But James and I were required to sign a release document *on any further claim to funds from William's estate."*

There was never any mention of the three slaves Joseph Knight gave me in 1840 as my personal property. Nor was there any indication of further proceeds from a plantation that had been listed as wealthy in the 1850 Census, the year before William died.

Life in Houma ended. I'd moved there with William as a young wife and mother, a bright future before us. I left with the heartache of immense loss, the struggle and strain to regain guardianship of my children from former in-laws, and a determination to bravely face a new future.

***

October of 1856

James and I had a joyous reunion with the children. We left the Parish of St. Charles, the Hahnville area, and moved to New Orleans. Dora 18 now, Fannie, 13, Reuben, 11, and William, 8. We had all endured a confusing and difficult two years apart.

***

Life took on more positive aspects; the children were wide-eyed with city life as compared to their country childhoods. I determined to find positive ways to involve them with art, history, and my family to strengthened the bonds of our lives. We enjoyed many events; musicals plays, Mardi Gras parades, street mimes.

Our home was a brick two-story on the corner of Canal and Gasquet, with stables and a *necessary* (outhouse) in the back.

My country clothing needed to be updated. The Goudy's Ladies', a popular woman's magazine, was filled with relatively conservative new pattern styles with to follow. I had taught Dora and Fannie to sew and help make our clothes. I designed common day dresses with short underarm seams, a shallow rounded dip at the waist-front, and a soft and full fan bosom.

The fabrics I liked were woven ginghams, calicos, or checks and plaids for day dresses. Other costumes I'd make in taffeta with a collar of lace or crochet for fancy occasions. The most notable contribution to fashion, however, was the impossible hoop skirt. By 1856 it had greatly altered the silhouette of a woman's wardrobe and called for yards more fabric. If I must, I will try to go with fashion.

***

Memories of my New Orleans girlhood

Our life has settled down and gives me time to reflect on the difference now from my early life in New Orleans. The city had many people coming from other places to live here by 1835. Father said they had brought an atmosphere of confusion to New Orleans with terrible moral, civic, and intellectual wickedness. I understand that statement as an adult, but it was contrary to the way I was raised and was why my father didn't allow his daughter to venture out alone.

If we were sick a doctor came to our home. If we needed clothing, a seamstress would fit us in our own rooms. I did occasionally hear the darker side of Quarter-life in kitchen gossip.

Activities of offshore pirates, like Jean Laffite, were fairly common knowledge and contributed to evil deeds.

I remember slave auction flyers posted on almost every street corner for the booming interstate commerce in slaves. Sadly, that market of human flesh increased the wealth of the South. I saw black chain gangs strung together as they were used to build areas of the city. They dug the drainage canals. Their slave labor paved our streets with cobblestone ballast from the ships. They moved massive amounts of earth on their backs to build the levees that protected the City from the Mississippi River.

* * *

When we returned in 1856, New Orleans was a rejuvenated city, transformed by its position on the Mississippi River. We were proud of our city had the nation's largest port. It was listed as America's third largest city, after New York City. Adventurers and immigrants filled the streets as they prepared to set out for the western frontier. Boats from the Ohio and Missouri Rivers passed New Orleans on the way to the Gulf.

Our family outings to watch ships move along the river, filled us with excitement. People took their leisure in Jackson square of an evening. Nearby we heard the noise and shouts of dock hands as they guided hundreds of ships into their designated areas. The river was packed with paddle wheelers, schooners, pirogues, and rafts. They sailed to the Gulf loaded with cotton, corn, sugar and hides for Europe, sugar to the English for their tea, downriver to Natchez and American fabric mills. Corn went to the Caribbean for rum, and on to the East Coast. It is still more amazing in my memory than I can describe.

Ships offloaded trade goods that filled stores of the Vieux Carrie with readymade clothing and numerous items for our homes. James and I often spoke of fortunes being made in shipping. Related commerce gave common workers jobs. Anyone who shipped products paid duties, so the area surrounding the Custom House bustled. Small businessmen in the community did well. James and I were ready to begin anew. By 1860 he was employed as an Overseer. He worked directing black street crews, or when needed, at the Custom House slave market.

***

New Orleans had populations in two fairly distinct sections: Downtown and Uptown. There have always been these distinctions. One infused by cotton and sugar wealth, with large homes along St. Charles Avenue belonged to plantation owners as city homes; the other, home to free men and slavers who manipulated life deep in the streets of the Vieux Carrie.

The Vieux Carrie, or French Quarter, called Downtown, is the main area for homes of the Creoles, Frenchmen, and Free Men. The Uptown area west of Canal Street is the Garden District where German, Jewish, and English settlers built large homes or lived over their shops.

With this burgeoning population, we found our previous fears of disease and pollution remedied. The city built private

St. Charles Ave. home

water and gas companies. The streets paved with ballast from ships are illuminated with globe gas lamps. The lamplighter goes from post to post as the street begins to glow in his wake. A most beautiful sight to watch. Also two new hotels welcome travelers and three ferries cross the river daily from Canal Street to Algiers in Jefferson Parish.

***

Family changes with Civil War reality

BEFORE ME,
of Orleans,
PERSONALLY APPEARED,

Witnesses, declared to me that
Theodora C. Knight, her daughter

In 1856 I signed permission for my oldest daughter, Dora, to marry George O. Hall. At 18 she was in love and ready to begin her own home. A few years later, in 1860, we celebrated our Fannie's marriage to Frank W. Brown at the Algiers Point Episcopal church.

Then the reality of Civil War began in earnest. Our extended family remained in New Orleans when news came the South seceded from the Union. Other Louisianans chose sides based on their personal situations. I was thankful to have my daughters and their husbands near me. I thanked God my sons were still too young then to participate in what was to come.

***

Many residents, not inclined to be part of the conflict, moved to Texas to avoid military conscription and loss of their slaves and property. Others left and went North. Those who stayed with us thought to prove their loyalty to our southern way of life by supporting the secession. Some couldn't leave. For those whose families were a part of the infrastructure of the City, there wasn't much choice but to keep on with daily living. Businesses, food markets, doctor offices, and schools remained open as they could and were needed.

On March 21, 1861, Louisiana joined the Confederate States of America. With the little I knew, I thought the world was going "mad." White male Louisianans quickly volunteered for service in the Confederate Army. From letters sent home later, most indicated they were in the fight up in Virginia, Tennessee, Arkansas, and Kentucky.

***

The frenzy of so many men leaving the City and marching off to war was frightening. I mourned as James joined the Confederate Army with the 3rd Infantry under Captain Bond of the Mounted Rangers. His example encouraged my sons-in-law, George and Frank to enlist too. They felt it was a matter of their "duty as Southerners." Fannie expected her first child, which made her separation from Frank all the more difficult.

As wives and mothers we could only wait and pray. There were parts of our hearts that understood our husband's need to fight, but also broke anticipating our loss. I encouraged my daughters to have hope facing an unknown future.

We believe Frank was sent to Camp Moore after he enlisted in May of 1861. It was a Confederate training depot near Baton Rouge. The location was chosen due to its relatively high ground, abundance of fresh drinking water, and being adjacent to the New Orleans railroad and to easily transport troops.

More than 400 soldiers died during training in that camp, the majority from various diseases, including the 1862 measles epidemic. Frank may have succumbed, as there was no further word from him. We never knew for sure. He never saw his precious daughter, Ella.

**

It did not take long before we who waited were in the thick of it too. War news heightened my own anxiety about James. We knew he was in a few battles before being captured. Eventually we received word he died in prison on January 27, 1862 of measles complicated by pneumonia. His friend and commanding officer had his body returned home.

How do I write these words with such seeming dullness of spirit? At least I knew when and how he died. Can I fully grieve the loss of a second husband with the tension of Union forces at our door? The care of my sons as our supplies run low? And comforting my daughter, Fannie, grieving the loss of her husband, Frank. It has all left me emotionless.

Then George Hall, Dora's husband, succumbed on May 28, 1863, just before the battle of Port Hudson from a wound in his thigh. By that spring of 1863 my daughters, Dora and Fannie, and I were widows. It was a senseless war. Our children and we were the losers.

We resolutely faced difficult days together. My life so far had taught me there are dangers for a woman without physical protection and legal representation. I hope the trials of my life will show my children how to be cautious and wise, but extremely brave.

**

Remembering Martial Law of April 1862

Dear Journal, I wish I didn't have to write *New Orleans has fallen to the Union Army*. The City surrendered without bloodshed, for that I'm thankful. Confederate General Mansfield Lovell saved the City from destruction as residents watched the local militia evacuate without a fight. His command included approximately 3,000 inexperienced and poorly armed troops to defend us. I can assume Union forces would have slaughtered them before our eyes.

**

By his actions though, General Lowell left the City undefended and put one-quarter of the state's total population, about forty percent of its white population, behind enemy lines. It made it impossible for cotton and sugarcane growers to continue planting and get their crops to market. Plantation owners had to change their thinking from being rich, to having no cash money even to buy needed supplies.

Despite New Orleans' status as the Confederacy's largest city and most important commercial center and seaport, it was poorly defended by Fort Jackson and Fort St. Philip, at the mouth of the river near the Gulf.

***

Horrified, I heard the news that Union Admiral Farragut had successfully navigated the lower Mississippi. It is shameful our Confederate troops stationed at Fort Jackson mutinied and then surrendered. This action secured the Union's capture of New Orleans.

Union occupation protected our beautiful city from the kind of physical destruction we heard other Southern cities sustained, but our living conditions were harsh. Our menfolk gone, a feeling of dread and terror took hold of our household. Each day we waited not knowing what would happen to us or to our city, or if we would hear from them.

On the evening of May 1, we heard a drum corps tapping out "Yankee Doodle." When I stepped to the corner, I saw Union General Benjamin Butler disembark a ship lying off the levee. He marched in step from the docks to the US Custom House. That day he began his short but notorious reign as the military governor over a scared and petulant citizenry.

This Union tyrant held us "captive" with his orders of martial law. I had never been "captive" to anyone before. My obedience to my father and to my husband was freely given. At one point, I thought of our slaves and their captive lives—no, we treated them kindly and cared for their needs—that's just the way it was for slave owners in the south.

None of our friends took kindly to marshal law. From the outset, New Orleans citizens treated Union soldiers with contempt and scorn. Women, in particular, verbally abused them, singing secession songs in their presence. They spit on them and dumped chamber pots from balconies.

***

Butler assumed the women also meant to "avoid contamination" with Union blue. They antagonized his troops by drawing their skirts aside if brushed by a Federal soldier. The deteriorating situation prompted Butler to issue his infamous General Order No. 28, posted in many places in the city.

Butler's punishments for these insults were "arrest, be held overnight in the calaboose and fined five dollars." Residents of the city did crack a grin when told what *real ladies of the street* did. Many flyers of General Butler's portrait had been distributed to the citizenry when he arrived. After the issuance of his *Women's Order No. 28*, the prostitutes pasted his portrait to the inside of the tinkle-pots in their rooms. Citizens had a good laugh when it was reported the General himself went to wield a hammer and break the pots.

General Order No. 28 by command of Major General Butler... "It is ordered hereafter when any female shall by word, gesture, or movement, insult or show contempt for any officer or soldier of the United States, she shall be regarded and held liable to be treated as a woman of the town plying her vocation."

***

Martial law under a tyrant is difficult to describe, especially since I had no experience being in a similar position. Thousands of our citizens, including slaves, were hungry and without means of support. Finally General Butler allowed troop rations to be passed to civilians and purchased some food for us with his personal funds.

The City lacked a functioning government. It was filthy and ripe for epidemics of infectious diseases. Crime was rampant with seditious behavior, including the threat of assassinations and smuggling. Eventually Butler ordered streets and canals to be cleaned regularly and crime rings broken up.

Before long the Union High Command in Washington learned how heavy-handed he was. They had to do something to keep the citizens of New Orleans from rebelling. Butler was replaced and left New Orleans seven months later on December 16, 1862. The *Daily Picayune* on that date covered the event in one sentence: *"We learn that General Butler and staff will leave the city at 10 o'clock this morning for the North."*

***

My daughters and I breathed a sigh of relief. I'd despaired under those conditions. I knew the City, but there were many dangers to face.

Father had died in 1849. My brother had gone—who knows where, dead or alive. Who could I go to? How was I to find a way to protect and provide for my family as a widow?

A tyrant was gone but the troops remained. A new commander came to rule over us. Our city was still occupied. Unprotected women had to be careful as they went to market or sent their children to school. Homes in the City were built close to the streets, with the smells, noise and constant threats of troops at our door. Our daily lives called for fortitude and courage. We needed faith that our prayers would be answered and we would be safe.

***

It was depressing to learn of battles our Confederate troops were losing. Our Confederate money also depreciated in value. By 1864, I was paying $5 a pound for butter; eggs were $5 a dozen; and milk cost an unbelievable $2.50 a quart. We found ways to use substitutes for much of our cooking and old-fashioned remedies took the place of medicines not available to us. Some cloth was woven and sewn at home. Mercy, can you imagine, our shoes consisted of wood, bits of leather, cloth and paper. The bare necessities of life were all that could be expected from our efforts.

***

Changes in 1865

The end of slavery was only one of the many striking changes to the home front in Louisiana now. Military-age white males had been killed. There was tremendous suffering from the disruption of the sugar and cotton trade, rampant inflation, lack of credit, and the presence of an occupation army. We Louisianans struggled to feed, clothe, and house ourselves. We faced starvation as Northern armies either seized or destroyed food crops. Then it was over.

How we cheered when the Union troops left. A new feeling of freedom was slowly reborn. We didn't have to hide or cower in fear of a knock on our door.

***

But what had we gained? We saw Louisiana soldiers, discouraged and ill, simply return home to begin the long road to rebuild their lives. But our family was not that fortunate. My dear James, Dora's George,

Fannie's Frank and other relatives had lost their lives for a seemingly worthless cause. My daughters and I used the abilities we had to sustain ourselves as dressmakers until the deprivations lessened. Fannie had married a Confederate soldier, during the war. He came home. There was happiness for them with their baby son, Reuben, and Fannie's daughter, Ella Brown, now 3 years old.

***

Commerce began afresh. Businesses opened their doors with the promise of rebuilding and the possibility of new hope to have cash crops and real money. The cotton and sugar industries, badly impacted by the war, were slow to recover. It was a new way of life as field hands were scarce.

Businesses and the way Southerners defined themselves for 150 years changed dramatically. Many people headed west. Northerners moved in and bought land that once belonged to large plantations owners and generations of Louisiana families. The South we once knew was no more. Antebellum was gone forever.

***

An overview of Fannie's life:

This tiny Southern lady's story has been told as a creative nonfiction personal diary. She married twice; once for love, once for protection. She faced widowhood twice. She bore five children, one died young. She confronted a patriarchal legal system and succeeded with patience and fortitude, to retain the rights to her children and their inheritance. She oversaw slaves as mistress of a large plantation. She saw the end of slavery, a lifestyle she'd known from birth, and adapted to it.

Frances Ann lived only a few years to witness the defeated South as a ruined land. New Orleans was becoming one of the nation's most rapidly growing metropolitan areas. She had been part of early migration from plantation life to the city. Between 1840—1865 an Industrial Revolution in America brought dramatic changes to the entire country. She saw candles in her home replaced by gas lamps. Political intrigue left her unable to comprehend the mental dividedness of those who would soon control the South.

In her daughter Fannie's memory book she left us a poem:
Oh no, I would not interchange,
For all the world could give –
The kind fond heart I love so well –
Where my affections live.
I would not sigh for pomp or wealth,
For what can e're they be-
To that pure love I know and feel,
Is centered well in me;
Oh search the mighty world around-
Can all it's power impart,
Or wealth ensure a gem so pure
As thy fond faithful heart.

By your Mother – Dec 31, 1869
      From Fannie's Album of Memory

✳✳✳

Frances Ann died at the age of 51, only four years after she bravely withstood the heartbreak and losses of the Civil War. She persevered under adversity in her short lifetime and left us a legacy of courage. She died of consumption (pulmonary tuberculosis) and is buried in Greenwood Cemetery, in New Orleans, Louisiana.

✳✳✳

The Next Generation

Her daughter, Frances (Fannie) Fredericka Knight Brown Farmer Mandell became the matriarch of our Louisiana family, living in New Orleans, for the next 53 years. The courage and faith she observed in her mother would steady her for many of her own trials.

Fannie's story is told in the next chapter through a recreated personal diary.

Jackson Square St. Louis Cathedral

FRANCES FREDERICKA
1843-1920

FRANCES FREDERICKA KNIGHT BROWN FARMER MANDELL

Fannie Brown

FAMILY CHART

Frances Frederick Knight—Brown, Farmer Mandell
    b. 1843—d. July 1920
    (1) Frank M. Brown—d. 1862
        m. June 7, 1860
            Frankella (Ella) Brown, Terwilliger—b. 1862—d. 1927
    (2) Sidney Leonidas Farmer—b. 1836—d. 1867
        m. July 1863
            Reuben Leonidas Augustus Farmer—b. 1864
            Almira Lee Anna Farmer Nick—b. 1866—d. 1938
    (3) Earl Mandell—b. 1847—d. 1925
        m. 1876
            Earl Eugene—b. 1879—d. 1946
            Jane Mandell, Thomas—b. 1881—d. 1937
            Frances Mandell, Roser—b. 1884—d.1957

CHAPTER THREE

This Southern woman, barely five feet tall, was born in Houma, Louisiana. She spent her childhood on a sugar cane plantation worked by family slaves. She lived to hold her great granddaughter, Elaine Lacoste. Her story is written as I envision it.

May 1862 – Union occupied New Orleans, Louisiana

Dear Diary, little Ella, barely a year old, is stirring in her cradle. My sweet daughter has no idea her father lost his life for our Confederacy. As I watch her precious face, my heart breaks. Can I protect my young child napping beside me in this occupied city?

Grieving Widow from The Civil War Art of Winslow Homer

I'd hardly begun to call Frank my husband when he enlisted. His death turned my world upside down. Each day my grief deepens. Not passed my 20th year, married only two years, a new mother and now a widow.

Silent tears run down my face. I'm mourning not only my loss, but also our city to Union troops. My inability to trust leaves me vulnerable to fear. My future is a bleak unknown veiled by this indefinite time of uncertainty.

***

Melancholy thoughts of my wedding day ...

Frank and I boarded the Third District Ferry at the end of Canal Street that June day. As the boat began to move into the Mississippi, we looked at one another and then back at Jackson Square, excited and nervous as we approached the landing.

The Mt. Olivet Episcopal Church at Algiers Point had been our choice for a simple church wedding. My uncle, Edward Stringer, suggested it to walk me down the aisle. As many young couples, we expected, with God's help and blessing, to live out our vows for many years to come.

Can it be our dream lasted barely two years? Our plans didn't include Union troops occupying New Orleans or Frank dying. *How do I go on?* Grief restricts my decisions, even with mother, my sister Dora and other family nearby. My emotions are churning like the Mississippi in the midst of a hurricane. The wind-driven rain with its violence is like the bitter sting of fear.

Union control of the City compounds my fears. I've heard General Butler's troops are grabbing any private possessions they want without regard for their owners. He's also become incensed by the attitude of our New Orleans ladies. I know they don't like the soldiers and insult them by various means. We are angry and lash out with words or actions, isn't that natural?

***

July—1863

Women have a very hard job in war – waiting – waiting for outcomes they fear and don't know how to predict. We pray for our loved ones, all the while maintaining a home to protect our children in spite of immense hardships.

Thank God Mama invited us to move into her home when Frank left and I was expecting our child. Now we've lost Frank, Mr. Bell (James) and George, my sister's husband. There hasn't been any recent word from other relatives up in Opelousas or how the fighting has affected them. Women neighbors are also widowed. God help us all.

***

Dear Diary,

If I think too long on my present circumstances I will be weighed down and tears will flow once more. So I choose to remember and write of pleasant times in my childhood.

My life began at home on January 3, 1843, on Bayou Black near Houma, Louisiana. I was named Frances Fredericka Knight, but called Fannie to avoid confusion with my mother. My oldest sister, Theodora (Dora) Catherine was born in 1838 in New Orleans. My next sister Corinne Elizabeth was also born in New Orleans in 1840, but she died in 1844. I was so young I don't remember her. My two younger brothers Reuben, 1845, and William, 1847, were both born in Houma too.

My Papa's brother, Uncle Michael Knight and his family lived near us. I enjoyed our school and Methodist church. I was a happy seven year old playing with my sisters and running barefoot on the cool earth of our sugar plantation.

I remember the dark, bottomland. When we children went in the fields, our slaves threw us short sticks of sweet cane to chew on. They cut the tall stalks almost to the ground to stack for crushing. We would watch the juice pour from the crusher into huge round metal pots where it was heated and stirred. Those pots sat on bricks over very hot fires in the sugar shed. We children were not allowed there, too dangerous. After the juice cooled we could carefully get a smear of molasses to lick and the rest of the thick syrup went to dry. Then it was packed for shipment.

Our plantation, I was told, contributed to the wealth of the whole parish. Papa worked hard to make it so. It made me feel proud to see hogsheads loaded for transport on the boats going to New Orleans. Mamma said some would go to people in England to sweeten their tea.

I remember how Mama and cook fixed delicious crab, red fish or oyster dishes. Fishing boats brought in plenty and we shared with our neighbors and they with us. Houma is still known for its spicy Cajun food, moist dark swamps, foot-stompin' music and country hospitality.

★★

Oh. How am I going to use the right words to explain a dark curtain that came down on my life and abruptly changed it? October 8, 1851— the day Papa died. I think Mamma said it was the terrible yellow fever.*

I remember the doctor visiting us and then he pulled a sheet over Papa. I was afraid. Mama was forced to let other people make decisions for us. She waited until Christmas to see if anyone would help.

I was 8 years old, but I remember how sad it felt not to hear Papa's voice. I would think he was calling me and then realize he wasn't here. I missed him at our dinner table and the times he took my hand to walk through the cane fields. Uncle Michael took us to the Houma Court House after Papa died to hear them read a paper to Mama. We were all so young; Dora 13, Reuben 5 and William only 3. Mama told us the court ordered Papa's property to be sold after the

*"The yellow fever epidemic of 1853 was one of the most virulent ever to attack New Orleans. Nearly 9,000 people in the city died of the fever between May and October 1853. John Duffy, Sword of Pestilence: The New Orleans Yellow Fever Epidemic of 1853 (Baton Rouge, 1966)"

harvest. They said we could stay in our home and have our slaves until June 1852. They knew crops still needed to be planted and harvested to have money.

That June harvest brought in no money. Mama never told us how she got any to take care of us. I didn't know all her problems. For a while she tried her best to manage the sugar production, work the slaves in the fields and watch out for us.

Then things changed. She married Mr. Bell. He was good to us, but there was a very serious issue in the law Mama didn't know about getting remarried.

She didn't know she was supposed to ask Papa's family first. She needed their permission to marry again. As I remember hearing, Uncle Michael didn't help her very much. When he was made our legal guardian we lived with his family for a few years while this was settled. It was a long time before it was sorted out and we could live with Mama again. I missed her so much and just wanted our family to be the same. We had lost Papa and now Mama too. Sometimes I wondered, after we left, who got all the things in our house.

***

1856—New Orleans

At last, this legal business in Houma was settled. I was 13 years old when we finally moved to New Orleans. I made adjustments to a new large school with children who spoke different languages, but I made friends. I enjoyed riding the wonderful new trolley up and down St. Charles Avenue and walking on paved streets. I had to wear shoes. Shops had ready-made goods for our home. Interesting people from different parts of the world owned the shops.

Before I was twenty-one years old, a lot of crazy things happened to me. I lost my Papa, adjusted to life with my uncle's family without Mama, moved to the big city of New Orleans, adjusted to a stepfather, married dear Frank, became a mother and then a widow. Trying to put my thoughts of these memories in a diary is difficult at times. Words aren't adequate. I'm thankful our family shares a tested faith that is a strong anchor for these storms of life.

***

1863—Grandparents

A sepia photograph of Frances Ann Stringer Knight, your Gramma, helps us see her likeness, a small woman in a simple, fashionable dress of the era. It is decorated at the cuffs with lace and a long row of round buttons down the entire front of the jacket. A special brooch holds a wide lace collar that covers her neck. Her hair is pulled back and parted in the middle with a braid that seems to be a decoration, as she usually wore it. Her high forehead, deep-set eyes and small mouth project a stern appearance but we know her as a loving person. Her face seems clear and unwrinkled.

My little Ella, I'm writing my thoughts today so you'll know what I was doing this warm, sticky day in September of 1863. We've been living in this wartime situation for several months now. Food is scarce. Soldiers are everywhere. Instead of fretting I'll tell you about our family. That brings me peace of mind.

I want to think of people who love and pray for us, like your grandparents. It is difficult to think of them when you don't see them and they aren't near you. You know Gramma Frances Ann loves you, but your Grampa William went to heaven over ten years ago.

I want to tell you about him, my Papa. He was born in Opelousas, a town north of New Orleans. His father, your great grandfather, was also named William. Papa's mother, your great grandmother, Christine Infield was from Baton Rouge. They lived in Opelousas and raised their family of seven children. Uncle Michael was the oldest and Aunt Louisiana the youngest. There were three girls, Tabitha, Christine and Louisiana, and four boys, Michael, Jacob, William and Reuben.

What we know of family stories goes back to your great, great, great grandfather, Philip Knecht and his wife Rosina Likens. They came to America in 1750, on a ship from Germany. Philip changed his last name, from the German spelling *Knecht*, to an American spelling, Knight. In Germany his name meant, "head servant." In America he was his own master.

They settled in Pennsylvania, in a farming area called Lancaster, near the city of Philadelphia. Other German families lived there and helped one another adjust to a new country. Philip was not a farmer, but a wheelwright. He made wheels for large wagons used to travel west and on to California.

***

Philip's son, Jacob Knight, your great, great grandfather brought his wife, Catherine Christine Infield, and their children, Solomon, Elizabeth, Henry and Joseph, from Pittsburg, Pennsylvania, to the territory of Louisiana. They were very brave to undertake a journey like that in 1798. It was roughly 950 miles from Pittsburg to Opelousas. They may have used a flatboat to cross the Ohio, Missouri and Mississippi Rivers. Catherine was 'behind a baby' (as they say in the South, to mean pregnant) as they made this difficult journey. That baby, born in Kentucky, was my Papa's father, William Knight.

Jacob bought land at Prairie des Coteaux in St. Landry Parish near Opelousas Post, an old French trading area in Spanish Louisiana. There they pledged allegiance to the King of Spain. I want to chuckle as I think of great, great grandfather Jacob paying for his land with cows. As the family settled in their new home, it's certain Catherine had a large garden. Jacob was a *chapelier*. He crafted men's hats from the plentiful beaver and muskrat pelts in the bayou waters of mid-central Louisiana. He traded them at the Opelousas Post where eastern travelers and European visitors fancied fur hats. Other settlers from France, Germany and the United States became their neighbors as this area grew. This is a story of our history in Louisiana, over 73 years ago.

***

December 1863

Dear Diary—In spite of this war, businesses still function. We need to buy food, care for our homes and attend houses of worship. Reports of battles the Confederacy have lost discourage us. My days are filled keeping my fingers and mind busy sewing clothing for our family and others. It takes skill to find goods for clothing. Although with shipping open on the Union controlled river, more are brought into New Orleans than to other Southern cities.

My biggest news is I recently married Private Sidney Leonidas Farmer, from Lynchburg, Virginia. He fought for the Confederacy with the 1st Alabama Infantry Co. D from Mobile, Alabama. He was captured at the terrible battle of Port Hudson near Baton Rouge and sent to the Union holding area here in New Orleans at the Custom House. He and

I met in that temporary prison when a few of our ladies took them provisions for comfort. Despite the difficulty of the times, a Justice of the Peace married us this summer. As I wait for his return we are expecting a new child to our family.

***

Holding Ella close and feeling a new life in me, brings a sense of peace that my faith will strengthen me through this waiting. I pray I won't be a war widow again. I am so anxious for Sidney to return. We share dreams of a safe home and large family. At present New Orleans is still under the harsh hand of martial law. Living here doesn't get easier, in fact, worse, but thoughts of a happy future encourage my heart.

I will keep this journal as a record of an historic and difficult time. South is fighting North, Americans fighting Americans. I am horrified by my feelings about the bloodshed and pain. Do "we the people" hate each other or is it the politicians who bring such horror upon us.

***

July 1867

Recently I became aware the Confederate army had interesting ways of using their troops. Men enlisted or re-enlisted for limited periods of time. In between enlistments they found ways home. Sometimes they'd sign up for a whole year, or sometimes a few months. If captured and taken to prison, they could sign they'd go home if released.

I will tell all my children someday, about the famous action Sidney took part in —the Confederate stand at Port Hudson, just north of Baton Rouge on the Mississippi. He told me 7500 Confederates held off over 40,000 Union soldiers for close to two months. They were eventually starved out, killed or captured, and surrendered on July 9, 1863. That was what brought him to New Orleans. Union forces

Sidney Farmer's Release Document

41

took their prisoners to our city until they could be transferred to the North.

In 1865, at the end of the war, my dear Sidney walked the 150 miles from his discharge point in Mobile, Alabama. He was so weak from long periods of fighting and being in two despicable prison camps but he gained strength with my love and cooking. He found work as a mate on a riverboat. Ella, you and your brother Reuben held a promise for us of a good life to come. Nine months after Sidney returned from the war, your sister, Almira Lee Anna, was added to our family in August 1866.

Sidney Farmer's Signature

Unfortunately, in a weakened state Sidney became ill and succumbed in my arms in March 1867. Now I am mourning again; the dark dresses, the loss of energy to focus on my sewing work. The recent stresses of the war combined with waiting for each moment we could be together, now gone, have taken its toll on me. Grief seems so much deeper. The closeness I felt with Sidney having his children and the relief he was back safe, gave me new hope. So many women lost their husbands, and children their fathers in this awful war. We were no different I suppose.

Ella, you never knew your father, Frank Brown, but you carry his name, Frank-ella. You were three years old when your stepfather, Sidney Farmer lived with us. You may have memories of his strong arms holding you tight. What a handsome fellow he was. When we met I was immediately smitten by his charm, good looks and Southern manners. He made me aware of his strong convictions about fighting for the beliefs of the Confederacy. As he left to go to a prison camp up North, he was willing to defend those convictions with his life.

Dear Diary, thank God he did come home, weary and sick only to succumb a few years later. Like you Ella now 6, Reuben 3 and little Almira Lee Anna not quite a year old, won't know their father either. In our four years of marriage I had not seen much of Sidney, but the heart is a funny thing. I followed mine to marry him no matter how much time we had. In the end, two wonderful babies are mine.

***

Dear Children—Ella, Reuben, and Almira—I remember thinking how New Orleans was taken over without much resistance. Why is this important to me now? We survived! Maybe you'll need to know someday how our beloved city fared during what could have been a terrible outcome. Conditions did drive us to our knees every day.

Enough happened in the hearts of our citizens during the awful Union occupation, to change them from enjoying lighthearted European ways of living, to war sick Americans hardened by the political greed that invaded from the north.

Antebellum New Orleans, was a place where people lived side-by-side, day-by-day, and enjoyed the freedom to live within their own cultures. Its lovely Spanish architecture, lacy balconies, and cool courtyards, combined old-world French traditions into a 150-year history.

***

1870

Can it be only four years since that terrible time ended? We were getting back on our feet and now struggle again with the recent loss of dear Mama. She was my rock when I lost Frank. She protected us in her home during the occupation. When Sidney died of the fever, she helped me with you children. I wonder if I will ever heal from these multiple losses in my life. I must remember that strength comes from our Heavenly Father and He never forgets us.

***

The wonderful year of 1877

I asked God to provide for my family these last five years or so as I combined a coffee shop with a boarding house. I enjoyed watching New Orleans come back to life, to its old ways of gaiety and friendliness. Our lovely city is once again enjoying the bustle of a thriving port where cargo and people arrive to be distributed to various parts of America.

In many ways the Northerners who came as victors caused us much pain. The confusion left us all struggling. Politicians tried to set up a new government system to include freed blacks. Many tricks were played on them with new redistricting laws.

But life goes on and I'm learning to adapt as I reach my thirty-eighth year. My recent marriage to Mr. Eugene Mandell made our lives better. He's a kind, distinguished looking, respectable gentleman who, after some struggles and changes in his own life, makes a good living as a house painter. He loves us, provides for our family and will be a good father to you young ones.

I am feeling very positive. This is a happy time in my life, in all our lives. I want us to remember and be thankful—not to only think of the hard times we've endured. I am so thankful for all my blessings. Especially, you Ella, my oldest 11 now. Reuben, 8 and Almira Lee Anna, 6. How I love you all. Your fathers would be so proud of you.

***

1880—Family changes

New Orleans in the 1880's, 15 years after the war, is a comfortable place to live: Operas to attend, street performers to watch in Jackson Square, café at the French Market and wonderful restaurants fixing delicacies from the Gulf. There are beautiful large homes along St. Charles Avenue in the Garden District with horse drawn streetcars along the avenue to the city center. By night more streets are lit with gas lamps, a pretty sight. The new Tulane College, along with public schools for children, brings more residents to the City. English is now established as the state language for all, even if a home language had been French or German, especially for the elderly.

Ella you are nineteen and left us to attend college in Manhattan. You lived with your Aunt Dora and her new husband John S. Earle. Then you married your dear Ira Terwilliger in New York and were the first to bless me as a grandmother with three little boys; Frank, Arner and then Ira Jr. Your life is so far away in New York I hardly know what it's about. I miss you.

Reuben is 16, a young man with dreams of his own, working as a painter with Papa Mandell. My sweet Almira is 14 you are a big sister to your new brother and two little sisters. God blessed me in this new marriage with Earl born in 1879, then sweet Jane Eliza in 1881 and Fanny Ann in 1884. How this was possible at my age, only God knows.

***

Dear Diary,

Fanny Ann married Gus (Gustave Philip Roser) in January of 1902. Reuben (Leonidas) married Elena 1901. Reuben, Mary Lena and Sidney were their children. Earl Eugene Mandell married Marietta and they have three little girls, Frances, Olive, Nettie. I enjoy all these little ones. Grandchildren are an even greater blessing without the worry of providing for them.

Almira married Mr. Henry Nick in 1885 in a small ceremony at our home. Their lovely family has grown to include Carrie, Ella, Hetty, Rowena, Henry, Georgie and Sidney who live near me. It's already 1917. I can hardly believe I've lived to see Rowena's daughter, my great grandchild, little Elaine Lacoste, here from Lafayette today.

We've had a difficult time recently. John Thomas, my Jane's young husband, died. They'd been married only a year. I watched her go through the pains I felt losing my dear husbands, especially Frank, when I was so young. She came to live with us and keeps busy helping others with her nursing skills. She is a caring daughter.

Fannie & Eugene 1918

***

January 3, 1919—my birthday—I am a very old woman

Our country has been in another awful war over in Europe. They say it's the war to end all wars. Thank God it's not in this country. I've seen enough war to last several lifetimes. Our world has certainly become a different place as I've lived the past 60 years. As a girl I never imagined people could fly in the sky, talk over wires to each other's homes, or go from town to town down paved roads in automobiles. Today machinery replaces slaves on sugar and cotton farms. Trains carry cotton and produce, replacing riverboats. New Orleans is cleaner with new sanitation methods that bring healthy conditions to our city. We hear music and speeches from our President on radio. I have lived to see a new century. That's a miracle!

As I feel the end my life is near, I think of a poem Mama wrote in my memory book all those years ago. It reminds me of how she spoke of love. I want to leave a legacy of love like this for my dear children and grandchildren.

***

Frances (Fannie) Fredericka Knight Brown Farmer Mandell died on July 3, 1920. She was 77 years old. She endured the ravages of two wars that personally affected her immediate family. She lost an older sister, buried her father and mother and two husbands, Frank and Sidney.

Married three times, she bore six children who lived. She left us a legacy of how to be a survivor.

MANDELLE—On Saturday, July 3, 1920, at 11:45 o'clock a.m., FRANCES FARMER KNIGHT, beloved wife of Eugene S. Mandelle, aged 77 years, native of this city. The relatives and friends of the family are respectfully invited to attend the funeral, which will take place Sunday, July 4, 1920, at 4 o'clock p.m., from the residence, 4827 Magazine Street. Interment in Greenwood Cemetery. New York City, and Gulf Port, Miss., papers please copy.

Mr. Mandell died five years later. He is also buried in Greenwood with his grand-daughter, Fannie and her husband, Matthew Jenny in the Jenny tomb. (Mandell's name is not on the tomb.)

Her daughter, Almira Lee Anna Farmer, Nick, Gruner, became the matriarch of our family in New Orleans for the next 19 years. Almira was my great grandmother.

ALMIRA LEE ANNA
1866-1938

Almira Lee Anna Farmer Nick Gruner

From Mamma

FAMILY CHART

**Almira Lee Anna Farmer—Nick, Gruner
—b. Aug 11, 1866—d. April 18, 1938**
    (1) Henry Louis Nick—b. 1865—d. 1911
    m. April 1885
        Almira Caroline (Carrie)—b. 1886—d. 1960
        Ella Frances—b. 1887—d. 1957
        Buleah Mamie—b. 1889—d. 1889
        Hetty Louise—b. 1890—d. 1968
        **Rowena Corinne (Nena)
        —b. May 12, 1893—d. Jan 3, 1993**
        Henry Hippolite—b. 1895—d. 1948
        George Lael—b. 1899—d. 1922
        Sidney Lee—b. 1900—d. 1957

    (2). Frederick Gruner—b. 1882—d. 1944
    m. 1914

CHAPTER FOUR

*I*n 1866, Almira Lee Anna Farmer was born in New Orleans as the Civil War ended. Her story is adapted from letters she exchanged with her daughter, Rowena (Nena).

***

August 1923

Dear Nena,

Marrying Fred, I can tell you, was the worst mistake I made in my life. When my dear Henry died so young I thought I could handle raising my last three children alone. I tried, but Henry really spoiled me, in our 26 years together.

I didn't know who would take care of us when he died. Georgie and the boys were a handful and you, my strong child, left for college.

How could I have been so foolish to remarry so soon? But Fred was a real charmer and my vulnerability must have showed. I had doubts later when I learned he possibly wasn't even single when he asked me to marry him. Knowing him through our family connections, I didn't take a good, hard look at who he really was. And the way he's gone through my widow's inheritance. O, God forgive me. Compared to my wonderful life with my Henry, I could weep.

I finally got up enough gumption to file a restraining order against him. Besides being lazy, not caring at all about my children and abusing me, I just couldn't take it anymore.

What a mess I've got myself into, and my health…. The doctor says my diabetes is compounded by my weight. I just stuff my face to manage my deep unhappiness.

All my love, *Mama*

***

Dear Mama,

I realize how unhappy you've been, especially with the New Orleans heat and humidity that makes you so uncomfortable.

So I'm sending a special blue dress for you to wear on your birthday to cheer you up. The boys might come over, or Ella take you to lunch. Maybe it will make you happy to remember how Papa always felt you deserved a special gift or piece of jewelry when your children were born. I miss him too.

Life is lonely without a father; you know that only too well. You didn't even know your father.

Love, *Nena*

***

November 1924

Dear Nena,

You have a care about my life and remember when it was enjoyable. I think so often about meeting Henry when we were young. He worked hard to become a well-known merchant in New Orleans. He provided us with a substantial home as our family grew. We had a horse and buggy. Nanny Feen helped with you children.

Our family enjoyed the local entertainments of this wonderful city. Operas, street plays, and musical evenings at home with Uncle Reuben playing his banjo with Henry. There was always noise, people, and goings-on to do.

I was treated like a princess compared to what is happening to me now. Would you indulge me some remembrances? I need to find a way to put perspective to my life and not be so miserable.

Love, *Mama*

***

Dear Mama,

Reminiscing from a unbiased perspective is difficult, so let me help you think about pieces of your story, as you told it to me. I remember some of it. Enjoy the memories, the good and difficult ones.

Your story began on August 11, 1866 in New Orleans. You had an older half-sister, Ella, and a brother, Reuben, waiting for you to join the family.

Thankfully the Civil War had ended. Your father, Sidney Leonidas Farmer, a Confederate soldier from Lynchburg, Virginia, returned home in 1865. I believe he was the one who named you Almira Lee Anna. He probably swooned when you looked up at him with your lovely grey-green eyes. You favor him so.

50

Unfortunately he died when you were six months old. I'm so sorry for you and all our family not to have known him. Three years later your Gramma Frances Ann died. She had been a rock for our family and other women widowed by the war.

But your Mama, now twice-widowed, proved to be a strong woman too. She protected you, Ella and Reuben in spite of her own difficulties. Those years after the war New Orleans experienced many changes to its southern way of life.

Your papa and Gramma Frances Ann were gone. Your Mama had two small children to care for and you were an infant. This meant a sparse childhood for you as the South struggled to come back from deep deprivations. There never was a record of a Confederate widow's pension for her. There wasn't much money in the state's coffers anyway.

In 1877, as you turned eight, your Mama's third marriage provided the only father you would know, Mr. Earl Mandell. Within a few years you had a new brother, Earl, and then two little sisters, Jane and Fanny Ann. I can't remember you telling me much about growing up with them in that busy home. You were quite a bit older.

Your mother and Mr. Earl had a long marriage, over forty years. That reflected a stable home for all of you as the City experienced a tenuous rebirth and then exploded with wealth and growth. This part of your childhood gave you a solid foundation of security and love, a place to belong.

New Orleans slowly changed from a busy, noisy, dirty port city into a lovely place with grand homes. You said you met interesting immigrant families and learned about their cultures. You always had a desire to learn new things.

***

I hope my reflections help you see yourself as a true Southern lady, beautiful and loved in spite of those first years of hardships and loss.

I know you especially love the *Vieux Carrie*. Your Grandmother Frances Ann lived there for a time on Bienville Street. At night a smoky haze hides those streets of the Quarter. Sounds of jazz along Bourbon Street mix with shadowy figures seeking other pleasures there. That made the Quarter a fascinating place, but not one where a girl like you would venture without your father.

The old cobblestone streets with French and Spanish names are reminiscent of the cultures that founded our city. We are fortunate to enjoy this captivating mix of music and foods from Haiti, Germany, France, Portugal, and Spain.

During your lifetime you've seen New Orleans blossom to became known as the Queen of the Mississippi. Our ancestors rode the conflicts of its historical change as it blended influences of early conquerors from France and Spain. You've had advantages in your life as it developed economically, socially, culturally and artistically around you. We have an amazing family heritage of German and English ancestors in this place. One hundred thrity-nine years gives you a claim to be a "daughter of the bayous."

Lovingly, *Nena*

***

February 1929

Dear Mama,

I am thinking of you today. I'm imagining you in 1882 as you turned 16 years old, a young woman on the brink of a positive future. The city provided many entertainments to catch your fancy -- street performers, restaurants, and best of all the French Opera House at Bourbon and Toulouse. It was a showplace that captured your love of music and theater. Unfortunately it burned in 1914 and wasn't rebuilt because of lack of funds in WW I.

The most famous party in town is our Mardi Gras—*Fat Tuesday*. You already know about a group of young gentlemen who organized a masked parade in 1827 to celebrate Lent. This celebration is from our French and Spanish Catholic heritage in New Orleans, a tradition you were born into and we both still enjoy —Carnival.

You told me you would go with your brothers and sisters to watch the parades and yell, "throw me something mister," arms outstretched to the float riders. They would throw strings of bright colored beads, toys or trinkets. "Catch!" they'd shout, *"Laisse le bon ton roulle."* (Let the good times roll!)

Now I have some time between my classes to think about and write a very special part of your story. Sit for a while as you read. Shed a tear if it helps. I know you like this one best, so:

New Orleans was a continental city and marrying well was important in middle-class circles. As a young woman of nineteen, you accepted the proposal of the handsome Henry Louis Nick. For three generations his German immigrant family were involved in the city as boot makers, clothing manufacturers —or bar keeps. Henry's grandfather lived at 1244 Magazine Street, located near an area where an influx of Germans settled.

The Deutches Haus nearby became a meeting place for German culture and parties with dances, language classes and friendships. You may have gone there with Henry for dances a time or two.

I learned it was formed to help destitute women, who'd lost their husbands, or children their mothers and or fathers, on the ships bringing them to Louisiana. These women with their children or children alone would be stranded on the boat in the river waiting for someone to help them or they'd be sent back to their countries.

***

Henry and his siblings lived with his father Charles and mother Caroline when he was young. But Charles disappeared after he traveled to Texas. He began another life. This family tragedy was concealed when his mother called herself a widow to lessen the social stigma of being divorced or abandoned.

Their home at 168 South Basin Street was on the edge of Storyville. Without any support from their father, the boys worked hard to help their mother put food on the table.

Love, *Nena*

***

April 1929
Dear Mama,

Henry Louise Nick & Almira

You must be having a memory of your first anniversary this month. April 11, 1885, was your special day. You may feel dreamy, sad, or lonely as I write about when you and Papa were married at home at 174 South Basin Street. You've told us this story often with a smile.

The church record lists your witnesses as Uncle Reuben and a friend, Edgar

53

Stonewall Raymond. Other relatives including your little sisters were excited too. Such a beautiful young woman you were and very much in love with 'your Henry' (as you always called him).

You told me about your first home on Milaudon Street—close to the river and to Henry's grandfather. There you began your life and eventually a large family, together.

***

I don't think you need to be reminded of your eight children, my siblings and me. First Almira Caroline, (Carrie) arrived in 1886, with Ella Frances a year later in 1887. Two years later, Beulah Mamie was born with birth complications and died within the month. The addition of Hetty Louise in 1890 grew the family to include three daughters and a Mama who seemed always, "behind a baby."

On May 12, 1893, I was born, Rowena Corinne (Nena), named after your great Aunt Corinne, who died as a child.

Finally, your first son, Henry Hippolite, (Brother) arrived in 1895, followed by Georgie Lael, another daughter, near the beginning of a new century in 1899. Then Sidney Lee stretched our household to include a family of nine by 1900.

***

Family stories are told that Papa provided you with gifts of jewelry and diamonds at the birth of each child. I remember mine was a wooden music box that played tunes on metal records. Practical and musical! What a thoughtful and loving husband. He worked hard to provide for us and show his love to us all.

Your observant focus was on raising us well. I remember you loved to memorize and taught us to recite poetry. Discoveries and visions of travel and history came alive as you read to us from the British Museum Handbook. You instructed your daughters to do lovely needlework, like Gramma Fannie taught you. Music, enjoyment of games and laughter filled our home. We were involved in the community too, especially with Papa. You were examples to us at home and at church.

You insisted we all finish high school. When the state of Louisiana made English the official language, you knew it was important for your children to speak and write it properly. There were those around us who spoke only French or Spanish. That didn't help them read documents or follow instructions. Many of my young friends began to lose the heart languages of their families. I think Papa's family still spoke German at home. Now only older folks do.

***

Our large family is still a bright spot in my own memories Mama. I realize at the end of the 19th century you were the wife of an up and coming businessman. We certainly needed a larger home for our family of seven children.

Magazine Street home

Our new home, at 4802 Magazine Street, was in the Upper Garden District (towards Claiborne and the new Tulane College). Remember the three-foot black iron fence and gate that "protected" the small front yard and low stoop from the street? There was a small porch across the front with two big windows to illuminate the front parlor. I watched you entertain Papa's sisters, Aunt Julia and Aunt Caroline, there. You used your good china.

The house was narrow, not shotgun-style as many in New Orleans, but rather deep from the street, with a tall second story in the back. We had a courtyard and carriage house behind where a smart looking buggy and sturdy horse were kept. On Sundays, Papa would hitch it up for special family outings to Hahnville in the country.

This courtyard had quarters for our nanny, Parthenia (Feen) Edwards. Feen also lived with Sidney and his wife, Irene, when their daughter Gloria was small. (This much-loved lady moved to a black nursing home near Lafayette and died there in 1939). Aunt Frances lived with you for a while after her husband Gus died.

I hope your memories include the games of pinochle we played with friends and how music filled our home. Other times Papa and Uncle Reuben would bring their banjos for a lively evening of hand clappin'. Carrie's ability on the harp added to our musical evenings. And Hetty was accomplished on the organ and played for silent films at the local movie theater. Remember she met her husband, Arthur, the manager, there.

'Your Henry' loved the ceremony of dinnertime and the kisses of his children when he came home. I insist he always said, "bread and butter vs bread and spread," when he asked for them to be passed at dinner. It

55

was a place of lively, happy family memories. They are surely wrapped around your heart.

Our life on Magazine Street was invested in a part of its long history as the center of old Uptown New Orleans. Markets, shops, restaurants and interesting homes are typical of the area now. Our home was near enough to walk the few long blocks to the St. Charles Avenue trolley Papa would ride to his store on Charters Street. Mama, you chose a man with a strong German work ethic. (I think I am very much like him.)

***

How you loved trips when he took you by steamer to New York, a destination for many residents of New Orleans as boat travel was direct from the wharf. I know you were delighted to accompany him when he needed to acquire materials, knowing we were cared for at home by Feen and Grandmother Caroline. Even Gramma Fannie would come to help, many hands were needed to care for seven of us.

To attend these events in New York and in New Orleans, Papa would insist you dress in lavish costumes with fancy plumes in your heavy chestnut hair. As a child I was interested in the dainty pair of opera glasses you tucked in the sparkly green-beaded evening bag you'd made. I'm happy you also afforded us opportunities to be involved with operas, musicals, music lessons and street shows.

The early 1900's were a time when new dramatic troupe companies came to New Orleans on large riverboats. German singing societies traveled throughout the state and along the Mississippi River Valley too. Music was everywhere.

***

"Myra"

Mama, to think of you now, a person on the outskirts of society, is such a contrast to the woman I remember attending meetings of different women's groups in New Orleans. I know you were a contributing member of the *Era Club, an organization in New Orleans for the furtherance of votes for women to relieve the injustices of men against women.*

I watched you march down Canal Street in 1912 with the Suffragettes marches. In the group picture taken that day you had a special pin you all wore on your lapels. I saw it in your jewelry box.

Were you involved in other social clubs before I was born? I am aware of a few that met in parlors and churches. Their focus was primarily on self-improvement and cultural activities. They read books, listened to lectures, and the ladies hosted musical events. That sounds like what interests you.

However, it was noted a change occurred in these gatherings as the social, political, and economic problems of the Progressive Era became increasingly apparent. Clubwomen turned from self-improvement to be more involved in national reform efforts. These efforts included, *the National Education Association, the Daughters of the American Revolution, the Women's Christian Temperance Union, the Young Women's Christian Association (YWCA), and the National Household Economics Association.*

I assume you were an eager participant. Those early clubs made a difference in the lives of women in New Orleans, especially for temperance, women's suffrage and efforts to rehabilitate prostitutes.

All for now, whew, that's a lot of memory.

Love, *Nena*

***

May 1929

Dear Mama,

I have some time today and thought of our family again. Those activities in your women's groups did not take you away from involvement in our lives. You were concerned with our education, our marriages, and later encouraged the boys in business.

You made it possible for Carrie to study the harp. When she moved to California, her new husband Joseph Christy, procured a special one for her. So sad he died while their children were young.

Ella met Raymond Squires while he attended Tulane University, near us. They married and also moved to California. Following the birth of their son, Raymond, and a move to the South, they divorced. After a serious accident, she married Doc Peacock, who cared for her. They live near you now.

Hetty married Arthur Jacob, from the theater. Their son Horace and his wife, Bootsie, gave you two grandsons, Ron and Jerry. When Arthur died she married Victor Meyer. Much later he passed and her third husband was Elmore Hebert.

Then there's me, your stubborn child. I was determined to attend college. You know my long story. I married in Lafayette while I taught there. Sadly Antoine and I divorced over awful circumstances. I made it on my own with Elaine for a while. Six years later I married Joe Pennock. We divorced after ten years.

We all left you. Georgie married Lewis Tally and had a son, Lewis Jr. who died in WW II. Henry married Eloise Cendon. Sidney married Irene Davis and their daughter, Gloria, joined our now extended family.

Your son's businesses stayed in New Orleans but they rarely see you. I understand men are naturally more involved with their wives' interests than their mamas'. But I do wish they would come to cheer you up.

You saw each of us on our way and remain as involved as you can by writing and visiting occasionally. Thank you Mama — I'm glad I can think of your love and care as I remember your life.

Love, *Nena*

✳✳✳

May 20 1929

Dear Mama,

These thoughts are for you, me too. I miss Papa so much at times. His is the special person I want to think about now. Make yourself a cup of tea and let your mind be transported to your happy days and happy thoughts. Okay? Settle down in a comfy chair.

Your Henry opened his own business as a clothing merchant in 1890. The store located at 1355 Camp Street, *Underwear Manufactures, Pinski, Nick & Co*, changed location a year later to 220 Decatur Street. Six years later disaster struck that building and his business.

✳✳✳

Times Picayune—Feb 12, 1896

Shortly after 6 o'clock last evening a fire, the cause of which is not known, broke out on the third floor of the four story brick building at 220 Decatur Street, between Customhouse and Bienville, extending to Clinton Street, owned by L. Blumenthal and occupied by Messrs. Henry L. Nick and H.L. Cohn, manufacturers of shirts and gents' underwear…the third and fourth floors were completely gutted, while the roof was destroyed and the stock on the other floors was badly damaged. ... the damage to the stock is estimated at about $5000 covered by a policy for $11,000. But the building next door caught on fire and the landlord allowed him to move to another building close by to continue his livelihood.

***

Papa employed 15 workers and participated as a strong influential member of the business community in the Quarter. He later relocated his clothing business to 319 Charters Street. He was active as a banker for the Woodmen of the World Insurance Company and served as a 32nd degree Mason. This increased his presence and made his dealings in the city well known. His company receipt said: BOUGHT of H. L. Nick MFG. CO, MANUFACTURERS OF LADIES AND MEN'S GARMENTS OF ALL DESCRIPTIONS.

***

I also knew Papa had other real estate holdings of 92 lots in what was to be developed as Evangeline City (Hahnville) near the lake. Each of his children would inherit a lot to build on, should we wish. I later discovered he invested in other in NOLA real estate and on Long Island in New York.

***

Your secure world and the routines of your fulfilling daily family life came crashing down when Papa had a fatal injury. His enjoyable relaxing fishing trip began badly. As he pulled the starter rope on the boat's motor, the tiller jerked back and cracked his shin. Over the next few days his wound became gangrenous. There was no way to stop the horrible infection. He realized he needed his short time with you to set his affairs in order and protect us. *(penicillin was unavailable then and only used for the military until after WW I.)*

He consolidated property in New York and New Orleans to eliminate financial worries for you. His death came in a few weeks on November 9, 1911.

You were 45 years old. Henry, Georgie and Sidney were still at home. Carrie, Ella, and Hetty were married and gone. I was to graduate high school the following June and desperately wanted to attend college. I was conflicted about my plans for an education. I knew Papa wanted me to go, but you ...

***

Death of One of City's Leading Manufacturers- -November 1911

H. L. Nick, for the past twenty-five years, a well-known manufacturer of ladies' garments and an extensive real estate holder, quietly passed away at his palatial home, 4802 Magazine Street, yesterday morning at 7:45 o'clock. The deceased was born in New Orleans, Sept 9, 1864, and received his education in this city. At (4.c) an early age he embarked in the overall and garment manufacturing business and at the time of his sudden demise the firm which bears his name is among the foremost in this section.

Mr. Nick is survived by his widow, Mrs. Almira Nick, and seven children, namely, Carrie, Ella, Hettie, Rowena, Henry, Georg(i)e and Sidney.

The funeral services will be held at the Free Church of the Annunciation, Race and Camp Streets, Sunday morning at 10 o'clock. The Masons will have charge, Mr. Nick being a thirty-second degree member. Aside from being a Mason, the deceased was head banker, Woodmen of the World, past chancellor commander Knights of Pythias, a member of the Grand Fraternity and several other social organizations. Interment will be made in Metairie Cemetery.

I know it's hard to allow me to go over this again Mama. I hope that with me being the storyteller, you will be able to weep, but lovingly remember the depths of your loss. Re-reading Papa's obituary notice helps me capture his finest qualities.

***

Whew, I need a deep breath.

Forever your life changed from one of middle class ease, enjoyable activities with family and the comfort of a much loved husband, to one of concerns for yourself and your children's future. Your grief was compounded by the death of Gramma Caroline Nick, just a few weeks after losing Papa. She had been a caring mother-in-law.

I can't imagine how terrible these devastating losses were to you. Not only did Papa provide for us, but we children knew how much you loved and cared for one another. I don't doubt this loss, this

H.L. Nick, 1911

sudden shock, must have brought up childhood feelings of your own fatherless home. Had you depended on Papa, 'your Henry,' to fill that hole in your heart? —*Nena*

***

A New Decade
June 1934

Dear Mama,

We've moved to New York where Elaine attends Bronxville High School. Joe is on the road again and I'm filling my time with classes at the Art Institute.

. . . let me tell more of your story now. That summer of 1912 after Papa died, I left for teachers college in Natchitoches. You always said, "Rowena you have your father's ability at business." But I left at a difficult time for you, a time where you felt very lost and confused. You needed help to keep your finances balanced, then and now it seems.

Your heartache, confusion and grief may have allowed you to believe the 19th century expectation "that a woman couldn't manage her own property or make good decisions." So, three years later on July 8, 1914, you chose to marry Frederick Jacob Gruner at the Free Church of the Annunciation. What was he thinking? What were you thinking? He was 31 and you were 48, with three children.

What confuses me is records show just two years earlier Fred married a 16-year-old girl following a compromising situation. I haven't been able to find any record of their divorce. There must have been extenuating circumstances you didn't know about.

As years went by your inherited widow's fortune dwindled with Fred's loose spending. I know you felt soon enough your decision was not carefully thought through. But who did you have to turn to? I think this new marriage after the shock of Papa's death alienated Henry and Sidney. Men can see through other men's tactics.

You continue to indicate in your letters Fred is a difficult man, a "heavy drinker and a sometimes worker." You waited until August 13, 1923, almost 10 years, to file a restraining order against him because of his cruel ways. You wanted him out of the house. Your petition listed "cursing, threatening, failure to support and provide, and desires a separation to keep him from harassing and annoying me."

Then, Mama, you let him come back. You attributed this decision to your "weak character and health problems." How could you do that? Was it only because you said you were uncomfortable living alone? Your need for companionship must have overruled your common sense.

More next time, I love you.—*Nena*

***

July 1934

Dear Nena,

I know you can't understand how vulnerable I feel. I presume I counted on having a younger man take charge of my life like Papa did. I felt so safe then. Now life has become confusing. I'm losing my grip on things. This city and Fred have become difficult for me

The Quarter is a gritty working-class slum. Even Jackson Square is over run by prostitutes using its surrounding hedges for their trade. I don't understand what is happening here. Your brothers never liked Fred so they stay away.

Mama

***

August 1934

Dear Nena,

We stayed in the Magazine Street house for four or five years before purchasing the larger home at 4419 Willow Street. Fred talked me into it and I spent $23,000.

That was the last straw. Finally I insisted he find a job. The railroad hired him. I will say it was nice to have RR passes to come to New York to see you, Joe and Elaine. But the railroad job was not stable as the Depression tightened the country's purse strings.

Now I am asking again if you could send us some money to pay our rent. We had to move to a cheaper place, half a shotgun, only $20 a month. Maybe the RR will hire Fred again and I'll come see you,

Mama

***

August 1934

Dear Mama,

After I married Joe I didn't come to New Orleans often enough. I apologize. I did not realize how difficult Fred and the city feels to you.

You cut your losses, gave up the big home on Willow Street, and moved to 1029 Arabella Street. You said "half a shotgun house for $20.00 a month, with room for Nena to come and see me when she can." The landlady pesters you for the rent and you asked for my help. You said Fred experienced many cut backs on his hourly wage job with the railroad so funds were tight. He was on half shifts or none at all.

Every industry struggled through the depression, but thank God Joe has hung on to his position.

Nena

***

September 1934

Dear Nena,

I am in bad health with diabetes and depend on my Nena girl financially from time to time to keep us in this tiny house. Your funds helped so much when the money wasn't coming in at all. I am no worse than thousands of others, the whole world is wrong. Read the 24th chapter of Matthew you'll find out why.

Mama

***

November 1934

Dear Mama,

I am concerned. Your life seems flat. The joy of activities and children is gone. You had such a big, busy household for so long. You had a life of music and attending events on the arm of a handsome, energetic husband. Now your life is so different. I try to understand.

Nena

Dear Mama,

You must imagine these days of meager resources as terrifying and disturbing as some of the hurricanes you've lived through. I remembered that one in 1915. It collapsed the Presbyterian Church on Lafayette Square and the St. Anna's Episcopal Church on Esplanade. Surging water from Lake Pontchartrain was forced into the city's drainage canals. So horrible.

Time to talk about some good things. Over the years you've welcomed seven grandchildren —one from me, Elaine, one from Sidney, two from Hetty, three from Carrie and one from Georgie. With train passes available from time to time you visited your daughters' families, and life seemed more bearable.

You went by train to visit Carrie and her family in California. I was pleased you came to Baton Rouge to celebrate my graduation from

Louisiana State University in 1926. By 1932 more free train passes allowed you to visit us in Washington DC and later in New York. We also appreciate these letters you write so often to keep in touch.

I know it helped when we sent your little granddaughter, Elaine to visit on her summer vacations. She usually stayed at Aunt Ella's, but as a loving grandmother you took her for beignets, a treat for you both. I thought when Ella and Hetty moved back to New Orleans they would be more supportive of your difficulties with loneliness. I know they do their best and love you too.

Love, *Nena*

***

November 1934

Dear Nena girl,

I didn't feel much like writing again for a while, as my health has really taken a toll on my thoughts and strength. Many of the letters I write to keep in touch with my children seem to have a somber tone. My life does not have any sparkle to it anymore. I made a huge mistake when I allowed Fred to move back into my new home, as he is lazy and mean. All I do is cook for him and eat too much myself.

I have such a bad cold, but like old Feen always said, 'if you go to bed, it just draws you there to stay, and you don't feel any better.'

I am as thankful as ever for the check you sent me and I know our God will bless you for it. I am enclosing Carrie's letter for you to read…I send my love to all of you, and a lot for my Nena girl.

Sincerely, *Mama*

***

December 1934

Dear Nena girl,

I am anxious for Fred to get back on the R.R. so I can go and see you again…we are very grateful for your check and Fred says, 'the Lord certainly is kind to us and I hope someday I will be able to return in a measure some of Rowena's goodness to us.'

Many thanks for Elaine's photo, it's splendid. Enclosed find a picture I've been keeping that is just what she looked like when she was just a little teeny, weeny baby.

Almira late in life

I spent a very happy Christmas as I had Ella, Brother, Sidney all here on that day with their wives ... only Hetty was not here, but she did not forget me as she sent me a gift by Ella. So I got shoes, slippers and a hat, which I sadly needed and I "took a treat" by taking Aunt Fanny (her half sister) to Canal St and see a show and had a nice toasted ham sandwich.

Today, Sidney took me to our bible class director's house to hear a (radio) bible lecture by Bro Rutherford and it was just wonderful the comfort it gave me. Of course it was over the radio from Los Angeles.

You wanted to know about Gloria, well she ...goes to the Catholic school. Sid told me today that she is revolting at things the Sister told her she must do and she said, 'I don't have to, you know my daddy is a *protistan* (protestant) and said I don't have to.'

Mama

***

Jan 14, 1935

Dear Nena,

... yesterday was Carrie's birthday, Jan 12, 1886. If only I could walk as I used to, I wouldn't mind it at all. But I can't walk, and two squares take all the breath I have.

I am writing tonight as Fred works late and I get so lonesome by myself. I just get to longing for you all to be with me. I only saw Brother (Henry) three times last year, he was here for Christmas day, said he was coming back, so far he has not come. Well dear may God bless and keep you all in my prayers for you.

Lovingly, *Mama*

***

Dear Nena,

I know you will be glad to hear from me and that I am feeling better. You know from Ella, I guess, that I have moved again and am living in the old house at 5209 Chestnut St. near Dufossat.

I am looking forward to you coming down here. Fred is back at work and it makes me feel I have a new lease on life. I expect I'll feel much

better as I have much ease in mind... I will say goodbye and God bless you my Nena girl,
Lovingly, *Mama*

***

Dear Mama,
You indicated that you and Fred have moved a few more times. Also Brother left you feeling dismissed. He lives in town and yet does not visit you very much, or as much as you would like. Does he still have negative feelings towards Fred? Remember I love you.
Nena

***

May 11, 1937
My darling Nena girl,
I still say I am thankful to God for my girls; they are worth double what my boys are. Excuse my writing as I find my sight getting so bad... Fred is now back on a regular engine. Thank God for that, I am worried as my ankles are swollen very badly. Dr. says it is my weight and I am inclined to believe him. There is no pain attached to it and I must remember I will be 70 yrs in three months.
Mama

***

Dear Mama,
Your letters are beginning to indicate the seriousness of your ill health. You forgot to even mention my birthday was the next day, May 12.
Nena

***

July 30
Nena, I am not feeling so good. It is awful hot, in the neighborhood of 95. I could write plenty but I don't feel well enough. Why don't we hear from you? I am suffering from the heat more than I ever did. Lovingly with love to all and don't forget Elaine and yourself.
Mama

***

August 11, 1937

Nena...this is my birthday as you know... three score and ten and I am awfully glad the Lord has smiled on me...Things are awfully hard but I am still proud to be left to my children. Many thanks for the dress, it is beautiful and just fits fine, and it is just my color for I love blue. I am glad that it is getting a little cooler at night.

Mama

***

Six months later:

Feb 15, 1938 — To whom this may concern; (The note the doctor sent to the family)

This is to certify that I am treating the wife of Mr. Fred Gruner for a very critical illness and have advised constant care and rest...Dr. Geo. Barnes

***

April 20, 1938
Dear Carrie, Ella, Hetty, Brother and Sidney.

I'm reading Mama's obituary in the Times Picayune.

On Monday morning April 18, 1938 at 4:45 o'clock, Almira Farmer Nick Gruner, widow of the late Henry Louis Nick and wife of Frederick J. Gruner; survived by six children of the former marriage, Mrs. Ernest Hayman of Burlingame, Cal. (Carrie), Mrs. Joseph W. Pennock of Detroit, Mich, (Rowena), Mrs. Cassius L. Peacock, (Ella), Mrs. Victor Meyer (Hetty), sons Henry H. and Sidney L. Nick of this city; (half)sister of E.E. Mandelle (Eugene) and Mrs. August Roser (Fanny). Internment in Metairie Cemetery, New Orleans, LA.

We are fewer, Your sister, *Nena*

***

Mama lived to see technological innovations including the telephone, telegraph, elevators, typewriters, phonographs, motion pictures, refrigerators, and washing machines. "By 1903 airplane flight and airmail service began. Everything was happening faster and linked previously isolated communities." (*US History Scan*)

Mama had been part of one hundred years of major changes in America. Earlier in her life she had embraced many of these new inventions, but as her health and mental sorrow increased, life pressed her down. I hope my review of her life brought her comfort as we exchanged letters. *Nena*

Almira LeeAnna Farmer Nick Gruner was interred in the H.L. NICK plot at Metarie Cemetery with her first husband Henry Louis Nick and his sister, Caroline Nick Attane and her husband. Other family members buried there are her daughter Ella Louise Nick Peacock and her husband Dr. Casissus Peacock.

***

Rowena Corinne Nick LaCoste Pennock became the strong matriarch of this Louisiana family for the next 55 years.

Carriage in the French Quarter (Adobe Stock Image)

FLOODING HITS NEW ORLEANS, 1926
PHOTO BY ALMIRA

Gramma said, "The flood was awful! We couldn't get out for weeks, so the vegetable man, the meat man, and the dairy man all came to our door in boats."
—Elaine

Rowena Corinne
1893-1993

Rowena Corinne Nick LaCoste Pennock

ROWENA N. PENNOCK

FAMILY CHART

Rowena Corinne Nick—LaCoste, Pennock
—b. May 12, 1893—d. Jan 3, 1993

(1) Antoine Wilbert LaCoste,—b. 1890—d. 1939
m. March 1917—div. 1927
Rowena Elaine LaCoste Adamson
—b. Nov 15, 1917—d. Oct 1, 2012

(2). Joseph William Pennock, III—b. 1904—d. 1962
m. June 1930—div. June 1942

Lace Balcony, French Quarter

CHAPTER FIVE

When you've lived one hundred years there's a lot to remember. I'm thankful I saved hundreds of letters from family and friends, diaries and photographs to bring these memories into focus to share my story with you.

I was told my birth on May 12, 1893 overshadowed the loss of my infant sister, Beulah two years earlier. I was now the fourth daughter of a middle class New Orleans merchant family. On July 30 that year I was baptized at our family church, the Church of the Annunciation on Camp and Race Street. Mama found my given name, Rowena, in her reading of Ivanhoe, an historical English novel. My middle name, Corinne, was in memory of my grandmother Fannie's older sister, Corinne Elizabeth Knight who died when she was four years old.

Mama felt it important for her children to attend services and be registered members at Annunciation Church. All our births, baptisms and marriages were dutifully recorded. My Grandmother Caroline Faulkenheiner Nick took us to her German Lutheran Church occasionally. It was similar to our Episcopal church, except I didn't understand German. One word I knew was *Koing*, which means king. A memory from a Baptist church I visited as a child was learning the song, "Jesus Loves Me, This I Know."

From early childhood I experienced the importance of faith in God as exemplified by Mama, not Papa. His Sunday morning was sacrosanct; sleep, not church.

My parents, Henry Louis Nick and Almira Lee Anna Farmer, were born and raised in New Orleans. They married in 1885 and by 1900 our large, busy family included seven children. Papa purchased a comfortable home at 1246 Upper Magazine, a tree-lined street in the Garden District.

Mama and my family called me "Nena," but to Papa I was his "Nena-girl." "Auntie Nena" to my nieces and nephews. Later, in college, my professors gave me the honorary title "Nicodemus." Social friends in Washington DC, New York, and Michigan called me "Penny" (Mrs.

Pennock). At Neumann school I was known as "Ms. Pennock" to students and then to their children I taught. To my four grandchildren I answered to Grammy, and then "GeeGee" (great-grandmother) to ten great grandchildren and five great-great grandchildren. I kept them all straight and answered to my various appellations.

***

In 1973 I wrote a letter to my great-granddaughter, Carolyn Elaine Smith for her 10th birthday. In it I described my childhood:

If you asked me what I did when I was 10 years old, in 1903, I should answer,

"When I was 10 years old there were practically no automobiles and the few that did exist looked very little like the autos we have today. Of course there were no paved highways, only shell and gravel roads from one town to another and no motels.

... New Orleans was special. We had streets made of rocks brought from Europe to weigh down the empty ships that came to New Orleans. They left the rocks with us and loaded on cotton and sugar grown in Louisiana. Also wheat and corn were shipped down the Mississippi River from Minneapolis and Chicago and St. Louis on riverboats and barges to our docks.

When my father went to work or my mother went to shop in the big stores they rode in a streetcar, which was electric but in towns nearby streetcars were pulled by mules. On Sundays and when my daddy took Mama to the French Opera they rode in our carriage pulled by our horse.

We children walked to school and came home for lunch and then directly home after school. Some neighbor children or friends came to play in our yard or we went to theirs but only with our mother's permission and only in the afternoon. Sometimes we had guests for dinner on Saturday or on Sunday after Sunday school.

In the evenings, after supper, we sat around on a large screen porch or in winter in the double parlors – like your living room – and we sang songs together. My father and my Uncle Reuben, Mama's brother, played banjos, one tenor and one alto...then my mother read to us - some of the poems she read were from the very same book I am sending you for your birthday - A Child's Garden of Verse by Robert Louis Stevenson. We loved the poems and learned many of them by heart." Love, GeeGee

***

A family tradition I remember was, "the oldest child did the buttons of the 2nd child, then No. 2 would help No. 3 get dressed and so on down to the baby. Feen, our nanny, took care of him or her." I feel I had an idyllic and secure childhood. We also saved our long hair from the nightly brushing to use as stuffing in pincushions.

A few years later we moved down Magazine Street to 4802 where we enjoyed the passing commerce of neighborhood shops nearby. Many evenings were spent on our front stoop greeting neighbors with a friendly word.

***

I was born into a growing city. New Orleans was one of America's busiest ports in the early 1900's. It was also home to incredible vice, on the streets, in politics and brothels in Storyville. A low standard of living that surfaced during and following the Civil War was rising again. Pirates attacked ships off shore, duels were held as common sport, and gamblers rode the riverboats fleecing passengers between New Orleans, Natchez and St. Louis. It was as if two or more distinct cultures coexisted on those streets in the Quarter and near the levees.

Not far removed from these dens of drunkards and prostitutes, lived hard working immigrants and law-abiding citizens. People of many nationalities found a touch of home in this multi-cultural city and became part of it.

My father's grandfather, Balthazar Nick, emigrated here in the mid-1840s from Württemberg, Darmstadt, Germany. He and his sons were skilled as craftsmen and merchants. They became part of a thriving business culture that was beginning to take hold then.

French sailors from the West Indies and Europe came to trade and taste a bit of home life in the Quarter. Jews came to avoid difficulties in Europe and responded to opportunities in business. Creoles, native-born French residents of Louisiana, intermarried with Europeans. Earlier, "Wild Americans" (Kentuckians) came to buy trade goods for their journey to head further west for land and gold. Former slaves and Free Men of color were integral parts as the city slowly prospered.

***

My schooling followed my older sisters'. I attended the same nursery school at St. George's Church on St. Charles Avenue. For elementary classes I remember the Berlinner School on Milan Street (after WW I they changed its name). The New Orleans school system in 1900 considered French culture and language an advantage. Until 1920 all documents in Louisiana were written in both languages, French and English, then that changed.

When I asked to go to high school, Mama made me go ask Papa for the needed nickel at his store at 229 Charters. That was the cost for the Magazine Street trolley. He said yes, I could go and could have the nickel. But I was often sick to my stomach on that car, so I walked, and bought a pickle with my nickel.

Small academic tickets I kept from 1909 -1912 to remind me my high school studies were in Mathematics, English, Music, History, Drawing and Expression, Science, Physics, Chemistry, Physiology, Economics and Civics. They show my good marks in school.

Graduation day from McDonough High School, on Napoleon and St. Charles Avenue, was on Monday, February 12, 1912, at 8 pm. The program I kept shows my part in the ceremony as a recitation of *The Waltz of Von Weber's. (Photo of McDonough High School grades)*

* * *

The Teacher

It was unusual for a girl in 1912 to want to attend college. My plans were almost derailed in the fall of my senior year when Papa died on November 11, 1911. We lost the strong leader of our family. His untimely death at forty-three, from a boating mishap, left our

Rowena with her young brothers & sister

entire family with deep wrenching sadness. His mother Caroline, my grandmother, passed a few weeks later on December 6, 1911.

I experienced overwhelming stresses when two of my close family both died so suddenly. A heavy burden was on my shoulders at seventeen. I was the oldest child at home. Since Papa handled all the business and family decisions, Mama enjoyed a worry-free life. Now I felt she needed me at home to help manage family affairs. Papa and I were close in mind and spirit and I'd enjoyed learning the business aspects of his enterprises. My lifelong passion for mathematics must have come from bookkeeping skills learned peering over his shoulder. My sense of responsibility for

Mama and my younger sibling's welfare filled my thoughts daily. *What was I going to do?*

It was a colossal decision to leave my family to follow my dream for a college education. *Could I have gone to Tulane down the street from my house? Did I want to prove how competent and strong I could be on my own? Did I want to run away from the pain of losing my Papa? Why did I choose to go?*

I covered my fears and grief with bluster. To others I may have seemed hard-hearted. Whatever life threw at me, I would hold on for the ride. I would not give up on life's problems without finding a solution. Stubborn and courageous defined me. Maybe this made me a good teacher.

***

My mother, my grandmothers and I were a part of the culture and values of New Orleans for over one hundred years. This decision to leave changed my outlook on my life. But I struck out on my own, and whether the choices were good or bad, they determined my future.

***

College days in Nachitoches were a breather from the grief and stress of the past year. Faded sepia pictures remind me of those days and my college friends. We played baseball in our long skirts, but dramatic presentations were my favorite activity. We took wagon rides pulled by stubborn mules.

Being on my own began to form a new strength in me. A dogged determination to succeed produced high marks. I was on a linear, arrow-straight path to become an accomplished teacher. I felt Papa cheering me on.

Nachitoches College Friends

***

However, in February of my second year, I was called to the dean's office. He informed me the Lafayette High School needed a teacher for a class of strong willed, unruly 7th grade boys. Having observed my tenacity, he felt my strength as a teacher could turn that class around. I agreed to take this difficult assignment. I agreed to go—*tout suite* (right away). I knew I would finish college in the future.

I hastily retrieved clothes borrowed by friends, packed and caught a train going south that same afternoon, 146 miles to Lafayette. A late start meant changing trains and also involved a stay over night alone in Carencro, Louisiana. This was not proper for a young single woman. It was impossible to find a room in a private home, so the stationmaster kindly suggested I stay in his office, which he locked. Safe and sound I slept on a hard bench until the train pulled in the next morning. I recall not getting much sleep.

I taught that difficult class at Lafayette High School until June. Exhausted I went home for the summer wanting to "retire" and change course. An offer to pursue medical studies at Tulane College would have taken my life on a different path, but Mama did not think it a proper profession for a young lady. She would not allow me to live at home if I pursued this course of study.

Heartbroken, unable to follow this new dream, I needed a job. I accepted one to teach English at Carencro High School. The following year I was back at Lafayette High School with a contract to teach Math and English. I taught there from 1915-1925.

I finished credits in German, Math and English missed by an early departure from Nachitoches, and graduated with a B.A. certificate in from Southwestern Louisiana Institute in Lafayette.

***

My capabilities as a proficient teacher were appreciated as I rejoined the educational community in Lafayette. I also caught the eye of Mr. Antoine Wilbert Lacoste, a local bachelor. He pursued me and left small notes of admiration in my teacher's box, signed Black. (His nickname because of very dark hair.)

***

1916 – one of his notes read:
Baby,
I have to go to Broussardville with Mr. Gunther of the Motor at 3:30. Sorry this came up. Will ring you on Teacher's phone at 4:30 and tell you about what time I will be back. Try to wait for me baby. I want to see you so bad. I love only you baby. Black

Our courtship had interesting twists and turns. Black came from a very large French Catholic family. His mother, Marie Euphemie Broussard Lacoste, a small French woman, never spoke much English. She wrote me notes and cards as my French was passable.

Euphemie Broussard's great-grandparents were part of the migration to Lafayette from LaAcadie, Quebec, in the mid 1700's. Later generations of her family felt privileged to contributed to the large Cathedral of St. John. Later generations are still numerous in the Lafayette and Broussard areas.

I, on the other hand, grew up in a large New Orleans Episcopal family where church membership drew very definite lines with regards to other faiths. My religious beliefs and church attendance were important to me and I refused to convert as a condition of Black's proposal. There was no one I trusted to advise me on this "bi-faith" union. I was away from my family circle, my trusted minister and Papa's counsel. When I said, *yes,* Black agreed to elope to Trinity Episcopal Church in nearby Crowley, Louisiana.

***

The Lafayette newspaper noted—

Lafayette Couple Put Over A Strong One On Their Local Friends

The fact that Mr. Antoine W. LaCoste and Miss Rowena Nick were man and wife since March the 19th last, became known to their friends no sooner than yesterday, after almost a month's time had elapsed. The event was kept secret for a spirit of fun more than anything else. The couple married in Crowley at 8 o'clock in the evening on March 19 at the Episcopal Church, Reverend Dr. Doswell, pastor, officiating. To hide his purpose the better, Mr. LaCoste drove all the way to Ville Platte, Evangeline parish, to get the license. He did this on March 17th.

The secret was let out when Mr. and Mrs. LaCoste went to New Orleans Saturday night and returned Sunday night with the announcement that they were married. Being surprised at first in

New bride, Rowena

the belief that the couple had been married on their trip to the city, their friends subsequently experienced a double surprise to learn they had been married almost a month.

Mr. LaCoste is one of the firm of LaCoste Hardware Company, of this city, being the bookkeeper. His bride is a teacher in the Lafayette High School. The many friends of the young couple wish them a long union of happiness and prosperity.

Another newspaper announcement: (same format as above)

… The news was kept a secret until this morning when they returned from New Orleans where they went to break the news to her people and spend Easter holidays. Mrs. LaCoste has been a teacher in the City High School for several years and will finish out the term, which will end next month. Mr. LaCoste is connected to the LaCoste Hardware Co. Both are very popular and have the best wishes of a host of friends.

***

The delay in our announcement gave me an extra month's salary, but the repercussions of the secret we'd kept were passed down through family stories. It seemed Black's family was not pleased with this match, even though they knew me as teacher to his younger siblings. His eight older sisters questioned his choice of a wife, outside the faith and Lafayette. This made our lives difficult. I was already carrying his child.

Yes, Black had eight sisters and four brothers. Many of them were married with families of their own. They proposed a way to breach this "gap of faith." If I could be convinced our child's best interest would be served if baptized at their beloved Cathedral, they would acquiesce demands for me to convert. When I would not agree, I felt his sisters turned against me for "trapping" Black.

***

He and I rented a little house at 301 Olivier Street while Black worked in the family business, LaCoste Hardware Company Ltd. It was owned by his father, Leopold and his Uncle Gustave, and located opposite the Court House Square and the Jefferson Theatre. They stocked "Buggies, Wagons and Farm Implements, Pipes and Fittings, Paints and Oils." Their phone was listed as No. 126, an easy one to remember.

One day the salesmen all went to lunch and left a boy tarring the roof of their building. The barrel of tar rolled and spilled catching the roof on fire. Everything burned and insurance coverage was not current. Black's father and uncle eventually opened a car lot on the empty space and did business there for many years.

Black took a new position with Lafayette Wholesale Grocers located on the railroad spur near Olivier Street, a quick walk from our house.

This new position required he travel with cardboard samples of caned and boxed food products to outlying stores for wholesale orders. These miniature items became a precious memory for our little daughter in her playhouse.

***

On November 15, 1917, we welcomed our only child, Rowena Elaine LaCoste, affectionately called "E-laine." My labor began the day I decided to dig a hole to replant an oak tree. The baby wasn't due yet, so I chanced my garden effort. Lifting the tree into the hole brought on birth pains. After a very difficult time, I delivered a little daughter with a long, skinny head.

Aunt Jane, Mama's half-sister, with her nursing experience, came from New Orleans to help with round-the-clock care for tiny Elaine. I remember peering at her asleep in my dresser drawer where I could observe her during my required laying in. As new parents we loved our beautiful, black-haired, twinkle-eyed little girl. We envisioned happy days of her growing up near her daddy's large family.

Black & Rowena with baby Elaine

***

In 1919, Lafayette had been chosen one of the few cities where WW I ace pilot, Clyde Pangborn came to perform. He dedicated his cross-country efforts to begin the airline business and champion the US Air Mail service. He offered residents of Lafayette a demonstration flight in his small biplane. Paying the $5 fee, I climbed in. After 10 minutes of barrel rolls and other tricks we landed. Breathlessly I asked to go up again. Delighted by my spunkiness he took me, this time free of charge.

I experienced a fresh surge of strength when I realized my own actions that day were ones of a determined woman. Mama and Gramma Fannie were my heroes. They showed me women could take control of their own decisions, thoughts, and life path.

***

Soon the on-going issue of Elaine's delayed baptism continued a family tug of war. The Catholic Church doctrine of infant sanctification was extremely important to Black's family. I found pressures escalating

81

surrounding this and other issues involving our different faiths. But I stood my ground too. My back was up, albeit quietly, and stayed that way for 5 years.

What eventually happened, as a result of this strife, leaves painful memories. I was caught off guard. My fortitude tested beyond limits of endurance. The antagonism caused me to experience a near break down from the stress. A Catholic priest mediated our stand-off. He felt I needed to make a difficult decision; separate from Black and move away from the overwhelming situation. There was a lot of pain and heartache to do that.

Rowena & Elaine, 2

I loved Black but could not live with him under those circumstances. He had not pressured me to meet them, but did not stand up to his family either.

It was 1924. I married late at twenty-four. I was now twenty-nine. How could I disrupt Elaine's relationship with her father and chose life as a single mother? I would need to work and care for a young child. I'd initially felt Black's large family would fill my life with the hustle and bustle of a big family like my own. It didn't. My own family was emotionally distant by circumstances of Mama's difficult remarriage. This decision was one of the most difficult I made in my life. I felt crushed and rejected. I took Elaine and left. I was on my own.

***

1924—Baton Rouge

A purposeful direction began as I enrolled at Louisiana State University for graduate classes. Education fulfilled my desire to be in control of my life. Elaine and I lived in a small garage apartment in Baton Rouge. We were close enough to Lafayette for Elaine to see her father and her beloved Grandmere Lacoste on special occasions.

We walked to campus each morning. This was a trying time for me with no real income, classes to study for, a child to care for and an unknown future. I believe my resolve to make this work grew new strength within me to produce excellence. I learned to not back down from challenges.

I'd envisioned a bright future when I left home to attended college. Now life turned out to be messy. I realized it was imperative to obtain a graduate degree. With the B.S. degree credits from Southern Louisiana Institute in Lafayette, I applied as a Teaching Fellow for graduate classes at Louisiana State University.

I manipulated my slide rule, the technology of the day, to solve difficult equations. I completed courses for two masters' degrees, in English and Mathematics. Seven-year-old Elaine, to her delight, was enrolled in LSU's early childhood experimental class.

Mama came on the train from New Orleans for my graduation ceremony in the new Greek Amphitheater on the LSU campus. As we arrived, the car door slammed on my fingers. I sat for two hours of speeches before I could tend to the incredible pain.

With the hard-won M.A. degree I also received a Professional Life Teaching Certificate from Louisiana and later one from Virginia. I was adequately prepared for our future. I felt proud. I had a vocation. I was an educator and I loved teaching Math.

Rowena graduation LSU 1926

***

I held a shiny "ticket" to new journeys. Neither a husband's wishes nor his place of employment constrained me. As a grown woman with a child and education completed, I needed a way to be employed. I chose not to look for a position in New Orleans near Mama, even though it would put me close to family.

Relief came in a simple, encouraging letter to head the Math Department in the nearby city schools of Monroe, Louisiana, beginning that fall. I breathed a deep sigh of relief. I would have financial stability. By January my direction changed entirely.

***

Warrenton, Virginia—1927

Virginia Odderstal, an LSU friend, wrote to me. After our graduation she had taken a position at the Warrenton Country Day School in Virginia. Soon a dashing Swedish Naval officer unexpectedly proposed marriage. This lovely turn of events required her to vacate her position as Head Teacher and Scholastic Principal. She thought I would be her perfect replacement. I accepted. Her recommendation and another from LSU secured the position.

Still considering myself a risk-taker, I couldn't wait to begin this new adventure. It seemed perfect, too good to pass up. The school would provide a place for us to live. I could care for Elaine and have a secure position. We were going North, to Virginia. I'd lived in Louisiana my whole life with a few trips to Texas. My horizons were definitely expanding.

***

Warrenton, Virginia

Our long train journey from New Orleans to Charlottesville, Virginia, began in February 1927. We traveled into a Northern winter. It wasn't long before we experienced many firsts. Pictures show our big smiles as we played in the snow in new fur coats.

We learned to ice-skate. I enjoyed my new life and responsibilities. Elaine not so much.

The rules at Warrenton Country Day School were under the strict control of Miss Lea Bouligny of New Orleans. She wanted all of my attention focused on the job I was hired to do. To counterattack, little Elaine got into lots of mischief. She suffered under punishments and demerits, which showed me I'd have to make another difficult decision.

Playing in the snow

I chose to enroll Elaine 75 miles away at St. Agnes, an Episcopal girls' boarding school, in Alexandria, Virginia. She was so young, nine years old, "so lonely" she told me in her childish letters for the next three years. She felt I sent her away to abandon her. I did. I focused on what I had to do.

Black and I quietly divorced in 1927, a most unusual occurrence in those days. For many years we exchanged stiff letters through a lawyer over the amount of alimony and child support. Black forcefully claimed I made more income and his payments needed to be reduced. The annoyance kept me continually reminded of the choices I'd made.

***

In the summer of 1928 I had an opportunity to do additional graduate work in "New Math" at Columbia University in New York. Elaine and I enjoyed some much needed mother/daughter time. She also attended a class for children. The big city gave us the opportunity to visit fascinating art museums and national historical sites. As I looked around, I imagined my parents visiting some of the same places on their trips in the early 1900's.

Elaine and I were expanding our boundaries and life experiences; Northern Virginia and now New York. I became acquainted with my Aunt Ella, Mama's older half-sister and her husband, Uncle Ira Terwilliger who lived nearby. Elaine and I visited their summer cabin on a lake in up-state New York.

I had a blind date, "a divine intervention," I called it, with a young man named, Joe Pennock. He held a solid position with General Motors. He said he found me a "lovely, determined woman very much her own person" and was smitten. He lived in New York City and I was teaching in rural Virginia. The US Mail service provided the "Cupid aspect" for us to become better acquainted.

Returning to Warrenton that fall, I felt intrigued with the possibility of a new romance. I taught my beloved subject, math. My position gave me the salary to keep Elaine at St. Agnes. This arrangement still worked for both of us, although at times I worried about her.

***

Europe—1929

I took Elaine to the Barcelona World Exhibition in Spain while we accompanied a few of our school's French teachers to Europe. We

attended cultural events in England, France and Spain that summer which sparked an insatiable thirst for me to keep learning new things.

Before we left Mama sent me the letter below with advice on travel:

Biarittz, France

May 15, 1929

Dear Nena,

I'm sending Elaine's papers too... The looks of them are due to the flood N.O. had when even

85

the canal bank vault was like a well (hurricane 1929). I was afraid to do more than dry them for fear of obliterating them.

I hope you have a nice enjoyable trip and return safe. I know you are pleasant company and that begets the same. I received your Mother's day message, many thanks….

Well I hope you and Elaine do not get seasick. I have heard to lace your corset real tight so as your stomach does not shake is a very good plan.

Well I can only pray you come back safe and all we can do is to trust that God will protect you two. I am as ever your loving, Mother.

***

A serious relationship was developing with Joe Pennock. He transferred to Washington, DC, and we saw each other more often. My position at Warrenton still gave me great pleasure. Elaine accepted her situation at St. Agnes without a lot of drama as she entered the pre-teen years. The friendship with Anna, her roommate, and her family, held her steady in rocky stumbles common to twelve-year old girls.

***

May 23, 1930—Joe's letter

Honey bunch,

All my time not devoted to business … might tend to make me a better companion to you mentally or physically… I was devoting myself to the worship of a person more perfect than I could even help to be, … because I love you and nothing can every replace that love in this life. Goodnight now Rowena,

Joe.

PS-18 hours from now!! You will be beside me when I go to sleep

***

June 11, 1930

Joe and I married in Rockville, Maryland, that June with a few friends in attendance. My post-wedding letter to Joe was written on a train while I took Elaine down to New Orleans for her summer vacation with Mama.

Joe and I began our marriage — separated. A pre-planned trip to accompany young ladies from Warrenton couldn't be canceled. Little did I know then we would be separated for much of our married life.

My Warrenton position required I accompany the girls into Washington, DC, for historical tours or musical evenings. I proved myself trustworthy and had opportunities to take older girls to Europe. I chaperoned President Taft's granddaughters on a grand European tour in 1930. We followed a carefully scripted American Express itinerary with a stop in Paris, to add high fashion to their wardrobes.

***

I resigned my much-loved position at the Warrenton School and began a trajectory of anticipated happiness; a future neither of us imagined. We found an apartment in Washington, DC, near Dupont Circle. I would be a full-time wife to Joe and mother to Elaine. She left St. Agnes and joined us to attend a nearby public school. Joe was back on the road as a claims adjuster for General Motors. I was anxious to teach, even part time, but he objected.

Joseph W. Pennock

My life as a married "stay-at-home wife" posed some challenges. It cramped my style. Joe didn't like the idea of me working, but he wasn't often at home. Teaching math was my life. It gave me purpose and challenged my mind. In spite of Joe's feelings and his ability to provide for us, I secured a part time position at Wilson Teachers College (1931-32) in DC.

There I met Bernice Angelico, a music teacher who would become a life long friend. When Elaine married years later, Beedee was her neighbor and a great help to the young couple. She would also be godmother to my two granddaughters.

***

1932

Joe was given a new position as an area supervisor. We moved to Bronxville, New York. President Roosevelt was promising a "New Deal for the American people." There was excitement in the air that the suffering of the Depression was over and American was on the road to recovery.

Elaine finished her last two years at Bronxville High School, while I enjoyed relaxed afternoons at the Art Students League. I'd begun early sketching attempts that garnered encouragement in high school. My painting hobby had flourished over the years.

Joe and I exchanged daily letters as he traveled around his large territory. He wrote of daily meetings and included many affirmations of his undying love. He assured me that even though he was away, he always thought of us.

Elaine graduated high school the same year General Motors moved us to their headquarters in Detroit, Michigan. We agreed she would attend the University of Michigan near us in Ann Arbor. By June, I was packing our New York apartment for a move to Detroit.

Joe had expressed concerns about Elaine entering a large university as an inexperienced young woman. To ease and protect her transition we decided to rent a small home in Ann Arbor and have her live with us that first year.

***

June 22, 1935—New York

Dearest Joe,

Elaine's commencement was all that it was to be expected, except—and a big one – you were not with me. Of course we understood, but we missed you just the same. As we planned, the packers will be here Monday and movers Tuesday. Elaine has gone to a party at Betty's in Scarsdale tonight. I've racked my brain to try to decide what was or is the cheapest way to get to Detroit and decided we better take the boat. And now to bed, with all my love,

Rowena

***

August 26, 1935 – from New Orleans

Dear Joe, My sugar,

I just received your letter from Cleveland... I wrote you after arriving here I did not find Mama so well. She isn't. She's too fat and won't diet or reduce. Dr. says that the pressure of fat around her heart is apt to prove disastrous almost any time. Saturday she had a bad spell and had to be put to bed with an ice bag – too much heat and a heavy breakfast and a feeling of excitement. I was planning to take her to Baton Rouge Sunday. She is better today but still weak. Ella says she gets these spells every once in a while.

As the time approaches for us to be together I get more and more impatient to be with my 'Honey.' Do you feel that way too?... Ella and Doc ... as well as Hetty and Vic are anxious to meet you and are insisting that we try to come down for next Carnival...I love you my sweet husband,

Rowena

Back in Detroit after visiting Mama, I was lonely. Elaine was busy with her college activities. Joe traveled most of the time. Our relationship through letters boringly detailed our daily calendars. Not much to build a solid marriage on. Thankfully the crash of 1929 was behind us. We were financially stable. What was I to do?

***

June 15, 1937– from Detroit, Michigan

Dear little Mama,

I think of you at least a dozen times a day... when I see a pretty garden of flowers or see a child do one of the tricks we used to try, or a hundred other things. . . .

Elaine completed her examinations last week and that puts an end to her first two years of college. Just think, she has reached the stage where I was when I first began to teach. Time flies. I am glad she has accomplished so much...

Joe, silent and sad, grieves the death of his mother. This week he spent Monday and Tuesday in Cincinnati and today and the rest of the week he will be in Toledo. Then home for the week-end ...

Nena

***

Occasionally I'd meet Joe in one of his layover cities. The local agent and his wife would entertain us to play Bridge or go golfing. Ho, hum! At least we were together. Or I visited Elaine on campus or she comes and stays at home for school vacations. Life was slow for me. I personally had no real focus. My confidence comes from doing what I am good at— teaching. There is feedback from my students. Others teachers seek me out. Daily I'd be in a social situation. Now, the days drag on.

***

April 1938

The next spring I spent the month of April with Mama as she battled the diabetes slowly taking her life. She died before the end of the month of complications of the disease. I was still the strong sister who made sure others were okay. But I appreciated the expressions of sympathy and lovely flowers sent by friends. They wrote, "There is no trouble so great that the understanding words of friends cannot soften." There was peace for my spirit in these words too…"It is wonderful to have faith that this is not the end – and that there is a Divine Providence that takes care of us all."

My strong feelings associated to my loss were later expressed in prose.

***

1939 Ann Arbor

Elaine began her senior year at Michigan full of excitement over progress in her voice study. Of course I could see this could not be a vocation for her. I counseled her to be prudent and consider other courses to provide a good employment later.

In the spring of 1939 she graduated with majors in French and Voice. Her graduation gift from Joe was a trip to France where she would continue her voice studies at the Ecole des Beaux Arts at Fontainebleau School of Art and Music outside of Paris. Joe indicated his concerned she not go alone and encourage me to go with her. I applied to fulfill a life-long dream to study drawing and painting. It was fun for mother and daughter, who had been apart many times in our lives, to share another exciting experience of travel, education and language. "We rode our bicycles along the river to school." "We had a *boulangerie* near our apartment."

A dream came true. My parchment document read: *Republique Francaise, Ministere de L'Instruction Publique et des Beaux-Arts. FONTAINEBLEAU School of Fine Arts, Palais de Fontainebleau.* Certificate of Attendance, to Mrs. Rowena Pennock, who has been a student in the school for a period of two months, during the 1939 summer season in the department of Painting."

***

As I accepted this diploma, my thoughts returned to 1910. At the age of 16, I'd begun to sketch with a mail-in drawing program. The reply to my efforts encouraged my talent. At first I experimented with little sketches, then took drawing lessons and art classes. In 1936 I invested in proper oil painting classes at the Detroit Art Museum.

Rowena Fresh Air Painting

In France, I had the joy of focusing on painting without other responsibilities. My favorite painting is of an arched stone bridge and Romanesque church near a small, meandering river. Women kneel by the water's edge washing clothes. The colors are soft, muted, and illuminated with light unique to France. This dream-come-true opportunity allowed me to paint, *au plein-aire,* in the French countryside.

Favorite painting

***

When our courses were completed in August, Elaine was offered the opportunity to continue voice lessons in Paris with a world-renowned instructor. We went to secure a job for her at a perfume shop to pay for her lessons. I planned to continue painting until we returned to New York, but to an unknown future. I knew of Joe's intentions for this trip when we left New York, but had not told Elaine. His letter arrived as we landed in France. I wrote Beedee after I'd read it.

***

Dear Beedee,

I don't know how to tell you how grateful I am for your letter with its expression of sympathy and friendship. And I don't know how to answer it. I am torn between a sense of loyalty to Joe, which I cannot deny as easily as he seems to be able to, and a desire for some kind of normal life.

For two years I have tried to persuade Joe that we have built up a rare association, companionship and understanding that we should not destroy, but he does not seem to want to see it that way. And so because I need to have an assured income he is making a divorce imperative.

Because of that feeling and my sincere affection for him I have tried to understand, …why is it he first said he loved Elaine more than me.

In fact that was the reason we were sent to Europe, with one-way passage during dangerous times and much against my better judgment, although I did not know it until I receive his 1st letter in France. He wants me to divorce him and release him of all responsibility for my support. He was insistent Elaine should have the trip when she graduated rather than later as I suggested. And Elaine, of course was thrilled with the idea and anxious to go then – so rather than let her go alone at such a time, I went with her having no inkling what Joe really had in mind. His first letter, written the day we sailed and received by us the day after we arrived in Fontainebleau, was requesting me to stay in France and get a divorce in Paris. You, who know how much I really think about him, can have some idea of how crushed I was…and still am…nothing permanent, nothing sure, nothing to be trusted.

"Penny"

***

August 1939

The rumblings of World War II were creeping towards Paris as Hitler made his move across Europe that summer. "I heard the boots hitting the streets of Paris" and decided we needed "to get out of here!"

My musings written at Fontainebleau indicate those thoughts:

"Day after day I saw the French soldiers march to their eastern bulwark (of the Maginot Line). They were poorly equipped, some men with muskets and helmets from the last war. Besides the daily cannon practice, we saw the French children go through their drills at the Cathedral of Chartres. Ten, eleven and twelve-year-olds would run up the ladders alongside the historical edifice and remove the glasses, practicing for the time when the Germans would strike. I'm sure when they knew Americans were coming, their hearts leaped with joy.

That the underground movements were and are working was evident. Everywhere in the cafes or in the countryside, were German tourists. These Germans were really German soldiers, the advance guard of the enemy. Even bicycles collected by the

French for means of transportation were waiting for the Germans and fell into their hands.

The American soldiers who remained after World War I and married French girls, and also American women who were serving over there are part of the backbone for the present French underground. They are the very roots and fibers of an underground system, the combining of American courage and the French desire to perpetuate France. The last picture I took of France told of the determination and love for their country."

***

Fontainebleau, France – August 1939

Dear Folks,

From my previous letters you had some idea of what was brewing in Europe. I was almost certain of the time and outcome, but I had Joe and Elaine's opinions to change on the length of our stay, hence we were nearly caught.

I stuck strictly to business and accomplished much— including a diploma in painting from instructors (Paughron, Maroget, Strauss and Nutherstellar) whose signatures and work stand for much in the European world of art. (I really didn't think I could do it) ....We had hoped, if we could stay on after school time, to spend some time in travel outside of France... Italy, Germany and England.

When August 24th came with its excitement and tension, I went up to Paris to see the situation through the eyes of the steamship companies and the American Embassy...

We discovered that the U.S. Lines were booked solid and the other lines were in a state of vacillating between sending and not sending their boats. Luckily we had not booked any passage back and therefore had our transportation money in hand to use at the critical moment. The steamship lines offered to take our money for a bed on the floor of any of the public rooms aboard but would guarantee nothing but passage. I wouldn't do business, but went again to the Embassy where we were advised to get to a port city and take our chances there.

Back at school (Fontainebleau) Elaine and all the young ones were still optimistic and not anxious to get out, but I finally persuaded Elaine to pack and get to Havre with me (the port of the U.S., French, and some English ships) and then if things blew over we could still do our traveling. It was lucky we did.

We left Fontainebleau on the night of August 29 – by then all the lights were blue-lit and ominous and the days full of soldiers marching to the Maginot Line – young, pitifully young, old, pathetically old, and a large grim, fatal, middle-aged group feeling the hopelessness and waste of it all, but determined to crush Hitlerism at any cost – poorly equipped, most of them having only one part of a uniform, poorly fitting shoes (signs all over asking soldiers from previous wars to bring their helmets if they still had them) and red-eyed but grimly working women in all the men's positions.

We arrived in Paris from Fontainebleau at midnight and went through dangerously dark blue-lit streets to our little hotel. By now the telephones were in the hands of the military and no telegrams were being accepted. A taxicab in Fontainebleau was found only after an hour and a half search by bicycle – as all cars, men's bicycles, horses, cows etc. had already been commandeered. In Paris, no porters available ordinarily, but that night, by luck, some and a few taxis. That was why night travel was best.

The next day we went again to the steamship lines. Many French, English and all Italian boats had been discontinued and there was no available space for sale on those sailing soon. So I made a reservation on the U.S. Harding sailing September 14th. Then after another visit to the Embassy, which by then was in a terrible state of crowded excitement, we registered our intention of going to Havre that afternoon and staying there until we could get passage, and also that we would register at the vice-consul there. You see we didn't want to be lost in the shuffle and leave no word where we were because of difficulty in all forms of communication.

Then back to the hotel (after securing a taxi) and thru to the station, where there were some porters, on a train as soon as it was made up so that we would have space for us and six bags, two paint boxes (I acquired a new one in France) a brief case of Elaine's music and two packages of my canvases and we were off to Havre. We evidently selected our times of travel well for on both trains we had all the room we needed, but friends we later met on the boat told tales of crowded trains and having to leave their baggage behind.

On the train we shared a compartment with a woman doctor, who with her doctor husband owns and operates a hospital in Rouen, a large city near Havre. She has two daughters near Elaine's age and she very generously offered us her hospitality if we encountered difficulties at Havre or before we could leave France.

At Havre we found porters and a taxi with less difficulty. It seemed less excited than Paris. The day before several large ships had left for America leaving a form of calm behind. After we 'loaded' in the taxi, we hotel-shopped. I had authoritative government information regarding hotels and what their prices would be so we avoided being detained. We found a reasonable, comfortable strictly French pension where we anchored, for how long we did not know. That night I slept very little and restlessly and was glad when morning arrived; then off to register with the vice-consul, which we did. While we were doing this a very large important-looking man came in and asked if the consul would advise him taking his family over to London for a week as they had to wait that long for their boat home. He was told the *Ile de France* was sailing that noon from Havre and he'd better get on it if he could - !! I beat that man out the door and not being able to find a taxi and not knowing which direction to go or car to take we got on the first street car (that was operated by red-eyed women) and were told where to get off and take the number – so-n-so to the dock, and we did.

French line luggage tag

When we arrived at the dock without the proper passes we had to talk and wiggle ourselves through three forbidden doors. By 11:45 we were standing next to a man, who after the proper persuasion, etc. sold us a cabin for two on the boat deck of the Ile de France. Then I stayed and cinched the tickets while Elaine went back to the pension for the baggage, which we had kept all ready in case of just such an emergency. It excites me terribly to relate all this.

And now since we are safely here (New York) we'll call this the first installment. We expect to be here until Sept 28 when Joe will be here on business. From there on I don't know what, but will let you know.

With much love to all of you, Rowena

P.S. I've just come across the copy I saved of The New York Times, Sunday, September 10, 1939 (headlines and story follow).

IL DE FRANCE HERE WITH 1,777 ABOARD

Most Passengers Americans, Who Left Europe on the Day War Was Declared

ALL FORFEIT PASSPORTS

Manhattan Sails Four Hours Late Due To Shortage of Seamen Willing To Embark

" ... Rushing across the Atlantic with her lights extinguished and her public rooms and cabins filled to overflowing, the French liner Ile de France, which left Havre on the morning war was declared, docked at West Forth-eighty Street after lying at Quarantine all night. She brought 1,777 passengers, nearly 400 more than normal capacity, and most of them were Americans who had rushed for accommodations when the clamor of approaching war spread over Europe.

The Americans who landed were the first large group to lose their passports under the new ruling of the State Department, officials of which have shown their determination to keep Americans at home, as least insofar as the war zones are concerned.

When they appeared for the usual immigration examination, passengers were informed that the State Department would retain their passports. They received landing cards as usual, and were told that for future voyages to Europe they would have to reapply for traveling papers. The Americans, glad to be home and away from the continual dread of a periscope sighted at sea, accepted this ruling without protest.

Officers of the ship maintained the usual silence, and passengers told usual stories of alarms, imagined submarines and wished-for naval escorts that apparently never materialized. The Ile de France docked on the south side of the French Line pier, across from the *Normandie*.

Among the passengers of the Ile de France were former United States Ambassador Walter E. Edge, Henry H. Curran, former deputy Mayor and now a city magistrate; the Grand Duchess Marie of Russia, Vladimr Golschmann, conductor of the St. Louis Symphony, and Gregor Platigorsky, cellist. Mr. Edge praised the liner's crew and told how the passengers had subscribed a fund of about 85,000 francs to be distributed among the crew.... The Grand Duchess Marie declared that from one viewpoint she was glad matters had developed as they did, because it had been disclosed that 'Stalin is as bad a dictator as Hitler.'

...The United States Lines began a program of partial secrecy, and will no longer give out all sailing and arrival hours. The European terminal hereafter will be Le Verdun, near Bordeaux."

NY Times September 10, 1939
Sales of Maps Soar Here

Rand McNally & Co, publishers announced yesterday that more maps had been sold at its store at 7 West Fiftieth Street in the first twenty-four hours of the European war than during all the years since 1918. The announcement said that fresh supplies of maps were being rushed daily by plane from factories working on a day and night schedule.

September 15, 1939—New Orleans

Dear Nena, Elaine, and Joe

You can never imagine how glad I was to get your telegram. I cried right into the telephone when Western Union read it to me...I could imagine all kinds of things happening to you both...When the Athenian was sunk, so was I. I am so happy and relieved that you are home I can hardly write.

Oceans of love and everything good from us,
Doc, Ella and Ray

***

War Years

Crossing the Atlantic on that voyage, with the tension and our vulnerability to the patrolling German U boats, kept us praying to arrive safely in New York. The war in Europe would escalate and soon involve all Americans in one way or another. Even the East coast was on alert for German submarine patrols. I saw concrete gun bunkers built along the beaches of New Jersey and Maryland.

That voyage was never forgotten. Our safety was a miracle. On our arrival in New York, I realized the distress I'd experienced on the ship was not solely due to the tension of the crossing. I received a diagnosis of a large abdominal tumor that would require surgery. At the same time I would also have to face Joe about the divorce he wanted and resolve our future.

I decided to receive medical care in New York. Elaine went on to New Orleans, her stay in Paris canceled. She needed time to discuss her plans with her Aunt Ella. Should she go back Michigan to begin graduate school or seek employment and live with her college friend in Washington, DC?

***

1940—St. Louis

Joe and I'd spent little time together in our 10-year marriage. Our relationship was broken. Joe's ideal was to have a wife at home with his child. After my surgery I was incapable of that.

Thinking I could salvage our relationship, I dutifully traveled to St. Louis where Joe wanted me to establish a home and wait for him there. "I'll finish up details," he said, and "join you as soon as I can." He still worked a very large territory and I thought he was suggesting he would be transferred to St. Louis. I found an apartment and waited.

I was exhausted from the tension of our escape from France and subsequent surgery in New York. I truly did not know what Joe had in mind in light of the divorce he'd already asked for. I felt fearful as I waited.

Inactivity was not my nature. So I began courses at university in St. Louis. I studied navigation, meteorology, and aerodynamics. These gave me a background for a possible job with the war effort.

Instead of arriving, divorce papers were served. Joe loved another woman he'd met on his travels. I was devastated. I had to painfully wait it out. Never one to sit and pity myself I went ahead and established residency in Missouri for the legal proceedings to follow. I had some seriously scary thoughts about myself for the first time in a long time.

Mama had been gone for three years. Until now I hadn't realized how much this loss had left a hole in my life. I wrote:

The Mother Circle
In trouble I feel so keenly the need of my mother – now a memory.
In sorrow, grief and confusion, I wish for her
And know that if she could she would be here to help me.

I feel alone, confused, deserted, uncertain
And think of death as a grand release and solution.

And then I remember my daughter—now young and sure and carefree;
On the verge of her marriage and so full of love and dreams,
Like those which now have fallen about the world,
That my sorrows seem not true or serious but far-away unreal visions.

And then I think:
I suffer now without that mother love and understanding
Because her time had come to pass beyond the veil;
If I now walked the path of least resistance
A time might come when she, my child, would need my hand or word
And I had been the means of keeping her from that
For which I feel the need so keenly now!

And then I think: Your life should not be finished
Till its need is over.
Rowena Pennock

***

In the meantime, Elaine' life had moved on. She went to DC, after a semester of graduate school, and in 1940, she met Keith. Her wedding was scheduled for June 6, 1941, in Washington, DC. She had met her true love. The lovely, simple affair was held at All Souls Episcopal Church. We had been the two of us for twenty-four years, now she was Keith's wife. She was moving out of my life, out of my control.

***

World War II—1941

WWII began in earnest in the Pacific with the bombing of Pearl Harbor that December 7th. The world truly turned upside down. War in two theaters. Goods at home were getting scarce. I watched American citizens play their parts salvaging iron that would build tanks. Saving and recycling paper, scrap drives to conserve resources, even kitchen fat and grease that would be rendered for explosives.

In early 1942, I was a new grandmother, far from my daughter and her new daughter. In March I boarded a train to Washington D.C. to meet my first grandchild, April Rowena LaCoste Adamson, named after me. My daughter, a wife of one year was now a new mother.

***

1942 New Orleans

Here I am. Three years of changes since I'd returned from France, and the world was going crazy. The whole country was on war alert. WW II was going global. Many changes had occurred for me also. When the divorce papers were finally signed in 1942, I returned to New Orleans licking my wounds. Single again, back home near a sister and brothers, I pressed on and played the hand I was dealt.

I found employment in the educational department of Higgins Aircraft Corporation as a Personnel Coordinator in charge of testing and training activities. This company built the Higgins Landing Craft used to land troops for D-Day at Omaha Beach. I'd contributed to the war effort.

***

Life Begins at 50

Prayers for direction and usefulness were answered for a new longer chapter of my life. Back in New Orleans I found a small apartment in a converted home on St. Charles Avenue. I happily accepted the challenging position in the math department at the Isidore Newman School, on Jefferson Avenue. I stayed 19 years, 1944-1963. I taught many notable alumni and later their children. Many had fond memories of Ms. Pennock and her math classes. I was tough and they excelled.

My life became dedicated to these students and I felt they admired me. I attended school functions—for sporting events, chaperoned dances, went to their weddings and encouraged them in their post college pursuits. Newman students and their families invited me to Mardi Gras festivities; balls and dinners. I enjoyed dressing lavishly in long gowns adding my fox shawl, long gloves and beaded purse. At times I was reminded of how Mama dressed for similar events.

I had the friendship of other teachers. We scheduled games of 'friendly bridge' on Friday nights. We enjoyed good food and occasional celebrations together in our favorite restaurants.

I usually found a good location to watch the Carnival parades and catch beads thrown by riders on the floats. Over the years I kept bags of them for my grandchildren on their occasional visits.

New Orleans is all about celebrations—Mardi Gras, All Saint's Day, Sugar Bowl football games and just any good time to sit and listen to jazz and have a beer. I remember my sixth birthday, a special celebration with Papa. He took me to Commanders Palace near our home on Magazine Street. My family joined me there to celebrate my 95th birthday. It remained a favorite place all my life.

***

By 1947 I had four wonderful grandchildren—April, Linda, Marque and Eric. At Christmas that year, my new double lens reflex camera gave me the opportunity to try out holiday photos. I sat them youngest to oldest in a row on the piano bench then and for similar photos as they grew up. A love for photography replaced painting as a creative outlet. It was also easier to transport and grandchildren needed to be photographed often.

***

My summers were free during my years at Newman School, so I indulged my love of travel to visit Elaine and family in their overseas posts. In 1950 I went to Egypt where Keith was attached to the American Embassy as Press Attaché. I enjoyed being a part of the French diplomatic lifestyle, even if just for a visit. At a reception at King Farouk's palace, our American Ambassador, Mr. Jefferson Caffree, greeted me from across the room, "Rowena, what are you doing here?" We were both surprised. I had known his family when I taught in Lafayette. We had a lovely visit that evening.

1958 Travels

During my tenure at Neumann, I belonged to the American Association of University Women, the National Retired Teachers Association and the American Association of Retired Persons.

Kids on a donkey in Egypt

After visiting Elaine's family in Istanbul, Turkey in 1957, I attended a conference of the International Women's Association of Teachers in Switzerland. Teachers in New Orleans appreciated hearing my report of the conference.

I was a careful, organized traveler, eager to try new things and meet new people even after I turned 70 years old. I extended a trip whenever possible to see other cities in Europe, but Paris was always a required stop when I was anywhere on the Continent. France held a special place in my heart from my first trip in 1927.

Other early memories were recalled as I shuffled through old tickets and ship's tags, from ocean crossings to Spain and France. Steamer trunks were used in the days you crossed the Atlantic by ship. They were large and had little drawers for folded things and a hanging section for your long evening things. Oil paintings on my walls also have shipping stickers on the back from the French Line, Isle de France.

In 1958 I was again in New York at Barnard College for the updated "New Math." I incorporated it in my classes until I retired in 1963 and later in South America.

***

Bogota, Colombia, South America

Not satisfied to be "retired-retired," I accepted a teaching position in Bogota, Colombia, at the multi-national, bi-lingual *Collego Nueva Granada*. My son-in-law, Keith, was assigned as head of the United States Information Agency for Colombia at the American Embassy. I felt excited South America would be a

COLEGIO NUEVA GRANADA
CARRERA 2-E No. February 7, 1958
TELEFONO 493-394
APARTADO AEREO 11339
BOGOTA, D. E., COLOMBIA

retirement adventure where I could almost live on the $321.00 I was paid each month.

My two grandsons, Marque and Eric Adamson attended the school. I wonder if they remember how strict I was? My position was to incorporate the new math into a regular curriculum for grades 1-12, and also instruct teachers to teach it. My responsibilities also included grading College Board Exams, as I had at Newman, for those students hoping to enter US colleges.

When my family left Bogota for a new stateside assignment I had fears of being left on the "other side of the pond." I remained for one more year insisting on experiencing adventures to other parts of South America. I was 73 years old when I returned to New Orleans in 1966. Old friends heartily welcomed me back to the social scene.

***

1972—New Orleans

Never the one to stop learning something new, I wrote: "I trained with H&R Block and counseled for them to coordinate TAX-AIDE gratis to deserving senior citizens. I completed the National Safety Council Defensive Driving Course and will teach this to members of Amer. Assn. of Retired Persons & Natl. Assn. of Retired Teachers who want to reduce their auto insurance premiums. I'm Treasurer of AARP for the next two years (should I live so long!!). I even added the time I spent as the original treasurer of Channel 12-WYES to my resume."

***

Home from Bogota, I again enjoyed the camaraderie at the Free Church of the Annunciation where my family had attended for sixty years. Serving on the altar committee or delivering flowers in hospital were just two activities I participated in to serve others and those of the church. It was important to me to be in attendance every Sunday, second row pew, right side, closest to the pulpit to hear the Bible reading.

Rowena, 79

I was moved to comfort my son-in-law Keith as he served at our embassy in Saigon. I wrote him, "I believe in God and Jesus Christ and I pray for your mental and physical well-being…"

1985—Life Changes

One evening I was accosted as I parked in my driveway by a man who came behind me and put a cord around my neck. I dropped my purse containing my $300 glasses, and he took it. I was eighty-three years old.

Growing older began to be a new reality. It was time. I needed help, but my strong will fought to keep my independence. I asked Elaine to come after I was also involved in a car accident that left me with a broken collarbone.

The home I carefully evaluated and purchased on Nashville Avenue had the main living rooms on the second floor. Taking those stairs, in and out, on a daily basis, I stayed in pretty good shape for the next eight years. The two bedrooms gave us plenty of room and the small front porch was an inviting place to sit and watch the neighborhood go by. Many homes like mine built, above a garage, took into account flooding that occurs with major storms in the city.

I insisted Elaine drive us all over the country to visit family. I didn't want to miss a thing or be bored. There was always something to learn or teach others. I belatedly met my great and great-great grandchildren. We attended special family occasions in Florida, Illinois, California and Virginia.

***

1983—Reflections

For most of my life I'd worked hard to earn my own money and support myself. I'd been careful spending, lending or investing what little I had when I could. These were lessons in thrift for those who learned it from me and for those who borrowed from me. I kept detailed books on every penny earned, saved or loaned with interest to others. I was the "family bank." Few paid me back but I kept close records on those pennies and nickels. I'm sure it seemed I exercised control over people I lent to. I did. Maybe I was conflicted myself. My reasons—I liked to control situations and felt safe when I was in charge. Thinking back was I generous or was it something else?

I followed the stock market ticker on TV daily for 50 years. Staying on top of the dollar was important to me. In the market crash of 1987, my fears got the better of me and I sold some long held securities like AT&T, Exon and Xerox. I didn't realize when my stocks rebounded that my portfolio was left short.

***

At ninety-five, I took a memorable trip with Elaine to Hawaii to visit my granddaughter Linda. One day as I stood near the water, a wave came over my feet, pulled me off balance and down I went. Linda came to my rescue and after a bit of gulping and drying off, I insisted I was fine. Those few exciting moments keep me feeling I was still part of the human race.

***

I remember a Mardi Gras parade when I was ninety-seven. My two granddaughters got my wheelchair to the sidewalk and pushed

me onto the grass at a good spot near the curb. I leaned my shrinking, frail body forward out of the wheelchair, held on to the arm of my chair and shouted, *"throw me something, mister, throw me something."* They did, I reached up to catch a shiny bauble as my childhood flashed back with all its excitement of life long memories. I felt like a child again as the "gift" came floating towards

"Throw me something!"

me.

***

One day I wrote reflections of my life. It seemed, like a cat, I had lived many different ones:
- Life at home with my family before I went away to college.
- When I went to teach in Lafayette and married Antoine LaCoste.
- Holding Elaine as a new-born and became a mother.
- At Baton Rouge with Elaine to complete an MA at LSU.
- Warrenton, Va. as head mistress of the Warrenton Country School.
- Married Joe—lived together in Washington, D.C., New York, and Michigan.
- Fontainebleau/painting. It turned out to be an easy way for him to take himself out of our lives. He was interested in someone else.
- Back to college classes and government exams.
- Readjustments to support myself again.
- Qualified for an Army Air Force position. At the end of war it directed me back to teach. More college courses at Colombia University.
- Teaching at Newman School and retirement.

• Then Bogota, Colombia, new adventures in South America.

I've had a long life. I am proud I kept my standards high, my morals strong, a dignity directed to be an example to my pupils – past, present and future.

***

Today as I tell my story I am a very old woman. I cannot sit or keep my brain idle for long. I watch shadows make shapes and angles on a wall. I comment to Elaine on their hypotenuse or diameter. As the world around me fades, I try to have conversations with people, usually insisting I'm correct on any topic. I look at *The Times Picayune* newspaper daily. A day would not feel right if Elaine and I weren't out and about in the city or driving through the countryside.

I leave habits of moderation as an example for all to follow: a small glass of wine or, sometimes a brandy after dinner, fresh oysters, Louisiana shrimp gumbo, pralines, and other Southern favorites, always the day revolving around some form of interesting food. I've lived a full, blessed life. Never in want, which wasn't easy, I persevered. I had a lot of fun too.

***

The End—told by Elaine

Early in December of 1992, at the age of ninety-nine, Mama fell on the floor of her bedroom. She was assisted by ambulance to the hospital to recover from complications of pneumonia. Somehow her shin was injured in her fall and the large bruise became gangrenous. It wasn't difficult for me to reject the doctor's suggestion to amputate her leg. Her injury was similar to the one that took her father's life.

I visited her every day, but soon realized she would not recover this time. In a coma for a month, and too weak at her age to fight the infection, she died at Turo Hospital in New Orleans on January 4, 1993. Her birthday would have been May 12, 1993. She made it to her 100th year! In burial instructions to the cemetery guardian I only said, "carry her gently."

***

In Memoriam, ma'am
by Elaine LaCoste Adamson, your daughter:

"Pythogoras died.
Euclid died.
Newton died.
Nena died… She's in great company!!
She smoked!! …maybe ten cigarettes, during an entire lifetime.
She drank!! …only before dinner, and, only sometimes.
She bathed every night…abroad, or at home, before sleep.
She never condoned, or used, bad language.
She expected, and searched out, the best quality of life.
She thought – positive – under all and any circumstances.
She was inspired by children, and, in turn inspired students.
She believed in God as 'mind', rediscovering in math and
science daily, in every kind of experience, a superior power.
She smiled to the end of a very long life,
content with loving all of us, forever.
Lovingly, your daughter, Elaine

***

Rowena Corinne Nick LaCoste Pennock was interred at Lake Lawn Metairie Cemetery in the H.L. Nick family plot with her father, Henry Louis Nick; her mother, Almira Lee Anna Farmer Nick Gruner; her older sister, Ella and her husband, Doc Peacock; two other sisters, Hettie, and Georgie; her brother, Henry Hypolitte Nick and her father's sister, Aunt Caroline Nick Attane.

***

Rowena Elaine LaCoste Adamson, became the next matriarch of this Louisiana family. She remained in New Orleans after her mother's death for the next ten years before moving to her daughter's home in Colorado. Rowena Elaine tells her own story in the next chapter from hundreds of her own letters and journals.

107

New Orleans Cabildo

ROWENA ELAINE
1917-2012

ROWENA ELAINE LACOSTE

November 15, 1917 - October 1, 2012

Rowena LaCoste Adamson

FAMILY CHART

Rowena Elaine LaCoste Adamson—b. Nov 15, 1917—d. Oct 1, 2012
    (1) Keith Earl Adamson—b. Dec 15, 1917—d. Oct 2001
      m. June 6, 1941—div. Aug 1969
      April Rowena LaCoste Adamson, Smith, Holthaus
          Linda Lee Fermor Adamson
          Marque Keith Adamson
          Eric Earl Adamson

Statue National Gallery of Art
Washington, D.C., photo by April Holthaus

CHAPTER SIX

In diaries and letters Elaine recorded her thoughts of people, places, emotions and dreams. The earliest ones from boarding school began when she was seven. Her last were memories written before she slipped away.

Her story is taken from 80 years of correspondence with her mother. Her journal entries and notebooks were filled with ideas to teach English for Non-English Speakers.

Elaine remembers an early life that began an inner struggle with perceived abandonment. A kind or loving touch often brought silent tears. As a child, she felt life was confusing; as an adult, at times it became overwhelming; and in old age, with its regrets, sorrowful. She learned to guard her heart. Then in her 80's she wrote poems of pain and confusion, joy and laughter that gave her courage to complete her life's journey.

***

Elaine's memories
1917—Lafayette, Louisiana

On November 15, 1917, I was born—ugly, I'm told, 6lbs, 2oz, covered with black hair and a squished head. Dr. Voorhies struggled for many hours for my safe delivery. However, none of the early tribulations of my physical birth would linger. Pictures show a feisty little girl with an inquisitive twinkle in her eye. My father suggested I be called Rowena Elaine Lacoste. The family always called me E-laine to avoid confusion with my mother.

***

Antoine (Black) Wilbert LaCoste, my father, pursued Mama with notes of affection left in her teacher's box at the high school. These affections soon led to a stolen kiss against a porch railing. After that breach of propriety they were married *tout de suit*.

Papa worked at the Lafayette Hardware Co., owned by his father Leopold and his Uncle George. I remember him as a shy, retiring person in my presence. I often heard him speak French with his family. He was well known in Lafayette. When I came to visit on school breaks, people always recognized me as his daughter, even on Main Street.

***

My Childhood

My daddy built a chicken coop-looking playhouse for me when I was three years old. It is my most precious memory of his love and kindness. He stocked little shelves inside with miniature cardboard cans of Libby corn, Heinz tomatoes, and small baking powder packages. I pretended, in my pretend kitchen, to cook in little pots and pans, feeding my doll. Daddy's old Ford sat beside it in our backyard at 301 Olivier Street.

An only child, I had few playmates. I liked having a little puppy to play with. My rules were *not to go out in the street, use bad language in French or English, keep my room and playhouse clean and learn my lessons.*

***

I knew French at home from my father and his family, and many others who lived around us in Lafayette. When I was not quite five, I would lift the phone earpiece on the wall and ask Lafayette Central to put me through to my Grandmere LaCoste. I would say, "please, I want to talk to my Grandmere." And the operator would say, "oh, 'tat you 'laine? Sor' honey, jus' a minute." Grandmere's caregiver Nanan would answer in French and my response was to say a few polite words to her first. *Bonjour, Nanan, comment ca-va? Oui, Grandmere, s'il vous plait.* All of *Grandma Lacoste* the nannies in my father's family, like Nanan, came from Brittany between 1865 and 1915. Grandmere had fourteen children. She needed help.

***

I have a dim memory of a few preschool days, possibly at St. John's Catholic Cathedral, that pleased Grandmere. Then I attended kindergarten at Southwestern Louisiana Institute, while Mama took classes to finish her college degree.

My childhood in Lafayette, safe with the love of my parents, Daddy's large extended family and familiar places did not last. Some of Daddy's family were upset mother had me baptized at the Episcopal Church instead of the Catholic Church. Difficulties between Mama, Daddy and his family became intense over religion.

It was horrible and sad. I remember hearing harsh words over these strange events. Differing beliefs fractured our home and their marriage ended in pieces. This was when I began to feel my life was not so safe.

Mama took me and left Lafayette. Left my daddy. Left my special playhouse. Left my Grandmere. I was six years old.

***

Baton Rouge – 1924-1926

Mama attended classes at LSU in Baton Rouge. A garage apartment near the campus became our new home. I attended the school's experimental preschool morning program in the old Civil War barracks, near the State Capitol building.

The teachers gave us lots of interesting things to do. One exercise I distinctly remember consisted of putting together individual words of a fairly long sentence. The words, printed in large letters on separate slips of paper, were disarranged on the table. We had to make a sentence from them. I enjoyed that.

After my class finished, I met Mama for lunch on campus. She got home two hours later. In the meantime I was free to do whatever I liked. I would wander the streets and pick up little "treasurers" off the ground and save them.

I was seven years old and away from Mama for many hours of the day. I missed my Daddy too. On Sundays Mama and I went to St. James Episcopal Church in Baton Rouge, it felt like a safe place in my life.

***

An Unknown Future—1926

When Mama graduated from LSU in May 1926, she received an offer of employment as head of the math department for the school district in

Monroe, Louisiana. She accepted the position, relieved and encouraged it would provide for our future.

In January 1927, our stability changed. Mama made a quick decision to resign. She told me we were going on an exciting train ride to the state of Virginia. We packed our trunks. After a quick trip to New Orleans for our goodbyes to my Grandma Almira, Uncle Henry, Uncle Sidney and Aunt Georgie, we headed north to a new life.

***

Elaine, a journal memory

A porter woke us sometime in the early morning, around Charlottesville, as yet no light. We dressed; I in a new fur coat size seven, in anticipation of a frigid northern climate.

Steam jets from the engine clouded the platform as the engine puffed off in the cold. The stationmaster met us, built a fire in his wood stove, and invited us to make ourselves as comfortable as we could. We waited there until the house on the hill opened for breakfast. Stretched out on the wooden benches in the station waiting room, we dozed and dreamt about the snowflakes we had just seen for the first time in our lives.

At 6:30 am we playfully scuffed the deepening fluff as we walked up to a white clapboard house. Inside were lots of things that interest hungry people in the morning. Afterwards, the chauffer and a big car came to take us to the school, our new home.

The school itself was in the country about a mile outside the town of Warrenton. I remember thinking as we drove through the towering main gates, "I hope they can be closed at night."

***

1927—A New Life

Mama began her position as teacher/administrator of Warrenton Country Day School, a fashionable boarding school for girls. We both thought it a perfect fit. I was happy. It provided a nice place for me to be with her.

As Mama and I settled into our rooms her presence helped me adjust to new kinds of people and their *Northern* ways. I remember pictures she took of me in my first warm coat, arms out-stretched as if flying. I was joyfully child-like that day as we played together in the snow on a sledding hill.

I have many memories of our first days at this school.

…a rich girls school, known for its emphasis on the French language. Excellence, the order of the day. Beds made "just so" with the covers tucked in Mademoiselle's way, and only after they'd been aired during breakfast.

Sounds of piano practice from basement cubicles invaded the gymnasium beginning early in the day. In the dormitory, accents of fractured French echoed down the scrupulously clean halls, into tile baths and sparsely furnished bedrooms.

Counting by today's standards, meals were sumptuous. One cook, Naomi, was a favorite of the girls; Mary, the other cook, spoiled all the little ones like me. She left a plate of newly baked cookies on the windowsill at ground level for us to reach.

In the dining hall I got plunked down right beside Mademoiselle, the austere authoritarian French proprietress of the school. She made sure I would behave. This meant I would eat everything including sweetened stewed tomatoes—without flinching. I could not understand the mixture of sugar and tomatoes.

Beginning in the morning, every girl was obliged to speak French, to the best of her ability, ALLLLLLL day. In the evening, before the assembled group, each girl had to make a report as to whether she did or did not follow the rules. Each unfortunate, like myself, had to say "almost perfect," meaning childish impatience had given ground to language inability at some point and the person had to resort to English.

Not commendable. Not allowed. Worthy of 'walking points', which meant that for every demerit point, I had to walk— around the campus… again and again. No wonder I have such strong legs. We had uniforms designed in Paris, by Chanel. The ones I liked best  were dark blue serge with a delightfully warm, smooth feel. They were cut like a suit with a false bolero-type jacket over a cream colored blouse of crepe-de-chine with buttons. These were for Sundays.

Two people who cared for us were gentle, for the most part. Ms. BB was the nurse when we–myself and the daughter of the Siamese Ambassador had chickenpox. Mrs. GG was the mother of a teacher at the school and kept the little ones like me company. She made us brush our teeth, pile our laundry neatly, and clean out all the drawers of our dresser each Saturday morning. She furnished us with threaded needles for our mending. She helped us with prayers during our emotional storms, unlike my mother, who was very strict with me.

***

September 1927—St. Agnes School for Girls

It was difficult for Mama not to favor me over the other girls or to make an example of my misbehavior. They would tattle on me and get me into trouble. Finally Mademoiselle decided that it would not be possible for us to remain. Mama would have to find another position.

St. Agnes School for Girls

So Mama decided I would attend boarding school that fall for second grade at St. Agnes School for Girls in Alexandria, Virginia, about 75 miles away. She would stay at Warrenton. By May, my security and our six months together came to an end.

Mama could not often visit me at St. Agnes because of her job responsibilities. So I began lonely years away from both my parents. It was 1927 and the times demanded my mother make a living for us the best way she could.

***

"Denial at Warrenton"—Elaine's Tears
The school that was denied me
Was something like a dream—
Good on the one hand, Desperately evil on the other!

Punishments seemed small
To an adult with long legs,
But something that looked big
To a child of seven, only.

It took the form of 'walking off'
The innocent sins of the day,
'So many' for being late to class
'So many' for 'no homework finished.'

And thousands of hours charged
Against 'resistance to discipline,'
Or using English and not French
As the language of communication.

Finally, the choice was: Endless
Sames, bucking the wall of rejection
By the teachers at that school,
Or, separation of a little child

From the 'rock' of love in the mother.
At seven, separation was equal to
What grown-ups label 'purgatory,'
And the little ones interpret as rejection.

The stripes of that lash never healed.
They flash and burn, even in poetic rhyme.
Only God's unfailing concern for me
Has made those early memories bearable.

Elaine LaCoste- age 7 memories
1927 to 1930
>   E. LACOSTE, ST AGNES School, Alexandria, Virginia
>   To: Mrs. R.N. LaCoste, Warrenton Country School, Warrenton, Virginia

Dear Mother,

I think I would rather take music than art. May I? Please. I have to practice 1 half hour at least. Oh, Please. Send me bedroom slippers, a few dresses, and a picture of you. Writing paper, a sweater and try to get some new games for us to play on rainy days. Anna has a game of Parcheesi but we can't keep on with that and Checkers. I'm doing well in all my classes. Anna and I are washing our socks when we take our baths...

I took a dose of castor oil last night. Had a close call after. Oh, please send me also Mercuricromoe and get the brand called Saftey Stain and some of the Spirits of Camphor quick because I have a cut and fever blister. Ring me up <u>PLEASE!</u>

Loads of love Elaine LaCoste

(On the envelope flap:) "Please send me a pair of black shoestrings for my tennis shoes.

Anna & Elaine

***

Dear Mother,

Please write I feel awful lonesome…Will you get me mittens and golashares. Oh, Mother, I wrote daddy for another raincoat because the one I have is terribly short. Oh gee, come see me or phone, please – oh, do something. I'm …..Elaine

***

My hair cut resembled a bowl turned upside down. That is, until the iron curler came at me to make a few curls on the forehead and touch my ears as if to make curls out of them. The results were either minimally beautifying, or left as awful with the comment; "Well, we'll do better next time. It's getting late. If we don't hurry we won't make it to church on time." That was one of those rare Sundays when Mama came to St. Agnes.

***

Summer 1928—New York

The next summer, when I was ten and a half, Mama and I went to Barnard College in New York City. We stayed on 127th Street, near Colombia University. She took extra classes to of the *New Math*. Of course, something had to be done with me, so I attended the Horace Mann School, attached to Barnard's Teacher's College. I still have a little ceramic pot I created…an awkward, lopsided example of childish art, but a lovely pale turquoise color.

One weekend Mama and I visited my great Aunt Ella. She is Gramma Almira's half sister and lives in New York. It was nice to meet more of my family. Sometimes I feel so disconnected from anyone related to me.

On July 4th, Mr. Joseph Pennock was Mama's blind date to Coney Island. I went too and ended up sick to my stomach on the subway coming home. Not long after that, Joe got a transfer with his company, General Motors, to Washington, D.C. He courted Mama and they married on June 11, 1930.

***

Jan 4, 1929

Dear Mother,

Listen, I don't want to take music if I have to be in a class with 5 year olds and do what they do. I am going crazy with studies, music, extra classes and I can't stand it, really.

Hoping you feel alright and are not in such misery as I.

Your beloved daughter, Elaine LaCoste. Anna sends love to you and me too.

***

France and Spain —1929

Mama took me to Eruope during summer vacation. She was chaperoning a few of her French teachers from Warrenton School. We had fun at the beach at Biarritz, France where we swam and I made sand castles. In Barcelona we visited the site of the World's Fair. Mama bought me a Spanish shawl. I draped it across my piano for many years. This was a special summer for me.

***

In my diary I wrote: "I was at St. Agnes, separated from my mother from 3rd grade to 8th grade. We were usually together in the summers except for 1930 when she married Joe. Too bad she had already made arrangements to take some students to Europe."

***

June 1930

That summer I stayed in New Orleans with Grandmother Almira at her big house on 4415 Willow Street.

When Mama returned from Europe, she told us some hilarious stories. In Rome the Fascist soldiers had pinched the girls so much Mama cancelled the rest of their days there and left for France. There, the pinching-business was also in fashion but not as brazen. The girls had ordered clothes to be made at Paris designers and were all agog over their fittings.

***

1930—A Stepfather

I was about to embark upon a radical new concept—family style living. I remember Mama told me over and over again, "you must learn to love Joe." I didn't know him yet, but it wasn't difficult. I thought he was dignified. He did not really spoil me, but was an ever-present help when I needed it. That's a hard combination to beat and a complete change from my previous situation of boarding school. St. Agnes became a distant memory.

Mama, Elaine, & Anna

And that's the beginning of the story of our family living in an apartment in Washington, DC, the summer of 1930.

***

My first real home in six years—

In my mind, Joe tolerated me, an awkward 13-year old, with bony knees, and teen-aged emotions. I was his first daughter and came already grown up. During those first years I can remember we were three, not two. I was not shut out of family talk about money or any situation that affected the life we led together.

Joe's finesse was very aristocratic, his love unquestioned. Mama had a hard time with that, because she urged Joe and me to love each other. When we did, she was covertly jealous. She never expressed that emotion in words to me. But, I knew, she had a hard time with her unjustified feelings.

Our two-room apartment at 1819 Q Street, N.W., near Dupont Circle, was very small. The living room big enough for my cot behind the couch. That was my bedroom.

The next year, we moved to a larger apartment at 1640 Connecticut Avenue, NW. The big living room extended the entire width of the building. My new piano fit perfectly. There was a little elevator like ones in Biarritz, the French called *le cage*. Our fourth floor home was heaven.

Our view included the old streetcar that ran along Connecticut Avenue. I could even see a corner of Rock Creek Park and, from our roof, the increasing number of airplanes that came in and out of Washington National Airport.

One day as Joe was going to work he saw a woman thrown from her horse on the Rock Creek path. As he approached to assist her, she admonished him, "I'm perfectly all right, young man." He recognized it was Eleanor Roosevelt, the President's wife. What a story we had at the dinner table that night.

***

I had two dresses for school as I'd always worn uniforms. After a while Mama was able to make others, but those first days in public school were burnt into my memory. I was laughed at as I got confused and lost my way in the boy's corridor of that large school building.

By February 1933, Joe was transferred to New York City. We rented a small New England style, two-story "doll house" for my last years in high school in Bronxville. We were close enough to take vacations to Copake Lake where Joe's parents had a wonderful cottage. I learned to paddle a boat that summer. We went to concerts in the Berkshire Mountains where we sat in a forest glade—a place of enchantment, of music and solitude.

***

1934—Ann Arbor, Michigan

I graduated from Bronxville High School in June and was accepted at the University of Michigan at Ann Arbor. Mama had the notion I was so immature it would be better if I lived at home. Then she could make clothes I needed, give me any tutoring if my subjects got heavy, and get me "ready to be on my own."

That summer, when it was time for me to learn to drive, Joe borrowed a convertible from the GM factory. The pink Cadillac was returned unharmed after Joe maneuvered me out of a situation with a large truck. What a story!

***

That next fall my parents needed to travel and participate in General Motors social events and I needed to learn to live without them. So I moved to the Helen Newberry Residence near campus. (We dated Thi Beta's.)

I participated mostly in activities that included good music. I was tested as to whether I could sing well, learn the music, follow the director's guidance, and not stick out as someone who wanted any special attention.

Our choir performances with the Philadelphia Symphony remain as sacred memories to us who sang under such fantastically advantageous circumstances.

***

My College Diaries

On my first day of college, a professor, taking roll, said, "Rowena LaCoste." I answered in the affirmative and was Rowena from then on. College friends nicknamed me "Row," but I was always "E-laine" to my family.

I kept a diary, neatly inscribed for each day, for four years. I recorded my social engagements with many gentlemen friends: to fraternity dances, for horse rides at the school ring or in the country, and to plays and concerts.

My college focus included anything involved with music and drama. I auditioned for plays, wrote plays and sang in them, much of this, simultaneously.

***

Monday, Jan 4, 1937 a Philosophy class reverie:

"There are times I feel unworthy and lonely: Daily life in college was pretty much the same until I made a terrible mistake. That's all my life has been, a mistake at the beginning and will probably be nothing but that, until its close. I inspire no confidence, no trust, no real love. I can do small non-intellectual things well. The virtues of a peasant or a servant are my character. I feel these thoughts will haunt me my entire life."

***

Today Mama and I went riding–Everybody likes Mama so much, they think she's my sister. Went riding after class too with Mr. William Kincaid, the flutist in the Philadelphia Symphony.

***

Wednesday, May 12

Up at 5:30 to hear the coronation ceremonies of the King of England, George VI.

***

April 6, 1938 to New Orleans
Mrs. Joseph N. Pennock — 8415 S. Claiborne Ave, New Orleans, LA
Dear Mama,

Philosophy is swell fun. Irving Coti and I still go out to lunch now and then. I told you about Father Welmuth didn't I? Well, he is a student of Logic here who likes beer and spare ribs, like we do. We get together for lunch now and then. I never knew I could like or respect a Catholic Priest before, but he is downright fun, and so logical about it all. It's really funny.

I hope you are having a good rest with your sisters. How's Gramma? Your extra-obedient daughter (beginning this semester), Rowena II"

***

April 10, 1938
Dear Mama,

Spring in Ann Arbor is the most wonderful spring anywhere. The roses were cut last week and today we have a blizzard.

I hope everything turns out all right down there with Gramma. Give them all my love, Goodnight, sugar, Rowena II.

***

April 18, 1938 – Gramma Almira died
Dear Mama,

Joe called me from Detroit last night to tell me Gramma died. I know I can offer you very little in the way of comfort because I would feel as bad if not worse if anything happened to you. My hope is that Grandma and Grandpa Nick are together somewhere, as they should be. The tragedy of it is over. Their love story begins again.

***

February 1939

Practically a whole year has gone by. Haven't written in my diary as much. Being a senior in college has its perks and its demands. I am looking forward to what is in store for my future.

***

February 4, 1939

It is said, "into every life a little rain must fall". For me it was a thunderstorm. My Daddy died today. I got the news as I was taking my mid-semester exams. The train to Lafayette would not have gotten me there in time for his funeral. So I didn't go. I wonder how I'll grieve for him in the future. I later wrote this poem:

"Coping
I had my father's death
To deal with, long before he died.
He died for me, when I was taken away to Baton Rouge,
And I was only 'five and a half.' After that,
I only held him in the half-circle
Of my short arms, for a few seconds,
At greetings, some months removed
In time, from one another".

***

June 1939

Dear Mama,

I'm a college graduate! It's a great feeling of accomplishment. Even though I was not an honor student, I squeezed by with the traditional moments of doubt, fear, triumph and astonishment. I look back on that world of academia as a time of growth. I can't wait for us to leave for Paris!

***

1939—France

Childhood memories from Warrenton school directed me to little streams that flow through the Forest of Fontainebleau. I went out often to explore them with a small group of art students. Sometimes we'd just walk near the old Palace; sometimes, rent bicycles and disappear into the great, ancient trees of the forest.

Fontainbleau transportation

I was studying voice and my lessons were given on the stage of the theater of Fontainebleau Palace. A statue of Napoleon III was in the lobby and you could see him from the stage. My voice teacher would tease me, "sing for Napoleon. Open up, hit that high note, the C#, straight on and hold it for four counts." Well I did.

Once as I sang out in full voice, one of the young sopranos from the Opera de Paris entered the back stage area from the Palace library above. She cried out, "Who is that? Who? Who is singing?" Everyone was so happy for me. I had hit, absolutely true, a high B flat, and held it to the end of the correct count.

Since I'd hoped to stay in France and continue my voice studies, Mama and I went on the train into Paris. A *Perfumeries'* sounded like the perfect place for me to work when I had time from voice lessons at the Paris Opera.

The next day though, at 5 am, we felt the measured footfalls of French soldiers in the street. I wasn't as upset as Mama, but we left a note of apology with final payment on our abandoned rented bikes and took all our possessions with us into the city. For the next 36 hours we focused on gaining a stateroom on the Ile de France leaving LeHarve.

As we finally fled up the gangplank the purser looked at our distressed faces and pointed to cabin #7. *Vous pouvey avoir celle-ci, pour deux.* (you may have this one for two)

Dressed for ocean travel

The ship almost did not pull away from the dock when the captain was informed his ship nor any lives on it would be insured if hit by a German torpedo. There were many tense days as the ship moved into the Atlantic on a zigzag course for New York to avoid German U boats.

My dreams of studying voice at the Paris Opera died. The encouragement I'd received from my instructor, Lucien Muratore, was not to be realized. When we arrived in New York, the seriousness of what I'd left behind turned my confused thoughts inward.

***

September 1939—New York, New York

The excitement of the New York World's Fair, only an hour's drive away in Queens, reinforced the relief of our arrival. We were alive and we were home. The fair turned my attention from days of worry to the possibilities of invention and industry. The exhibits were stupendous, gigantic, with moving-parts, color, and lights. Food was available in hand-held paper containers so you could eat and keep moving.

***

September 1939

Dear Mr. Kincaid of the Philadelphia Symphony,

I have just returned from the American Conservatory at Fontainebleau and am trying to decide what to do next year. I thought you could help me.

As you know I received my BA in French and my teacher's certificate in June. You remember when we met I told you I was studying voice at Michigan. Then my family gave me a trip to Europe. This summer I studied under Lucien Muratore at Fontainebleau. Anyway, he made me promise to continue my study whether I did it with him or with someone else. After a lot of muddling decisions I decided to stay and go to his school in Paris, which would have been wonderful. One of the main things, that made me think he really believed all the things he said, was he asked Camille Decreue, head of his conservatory this summer, to hear me.

But history intervened – Hitler arrived near Paris and I left as quickly as possible. So here I am safely back in New York with different opportunity, the money and the desire to study voice with a lot of hopes and indecision. Or no. Could you advise me?

Rowena LaCoste

***

January 1940

I needed some perspective for my future, so I spent that fall and Christmas with Aunt Ella and Uncle Doc in New Orleans. They were so kind. They helped me see my place in the world as a grown woman capable of making my own decisions. Mama was not with me, but I knew she wanted me to focus on academics not voice. I struggled to determine if this was my life's true direction—what I wanted. Could I go against her?

This film opened in New Orleans before I headed north.

*Gone With the Wind
previewed January 1940*

***

Dear Mama,

Left New Orleans and slept most of the night on the bus, changed buses in Chicago and got to Ann Arbor by 7:00 am Thursday. Went to head of Graduate School, was admitted. Went to movies with Phil Saturday, class on Monday was pretty good.

I looked for an apartment all week. Almost took one today at $35 a month. Guess I can stand living at 433 Maynard Street paying $4 a week with another girl.

Irving is here, prosperous and still in love. Am fairly happy. Lost all the weight I gained in France, am 111 lbs. now. I am well and studying. Have graduate intelligence test today, also swimming meet. Love, *Rowena*

***

May 30, 1940—Michigan

Dear Mom,

Not until these last months have I begun to feel like all my parts are working. ... You know, as well as I do, the therapy of feeling like you're really doing something. And thinking, trying to work things out, going places, reading—there's nothing like it. Uncle Doc was right. I didn't grow up very fast, but he thinks I am growing in the right direction. I have started to realize my life will be full of books and news clippings and a few records, songs and poems, writing and painting and reading in French. I hope to be molded into some sort of a character of a lifetime of scholarly application.

Love, *Rowena (Elaine)*

***

June 1940 — Time to move on

Dear Mother,

I stayed in Ann Arbor until last Friday. I went to Senior Ball with Phil, and we went swimming out at Loch Alpine afterward. Long talks. Phil is dead bent on being a JD in the upper third of his class. I am proud of him too.

I can't get the spirit worked up in French, even after being in France. I got a C to go with the two B's, which means that I won't finish my master's in French.

I bought a lovely, little brass-enameled box to put my good jewelry in. It is sweet and blue and pink with green flower design, Chinese and very prim and demure looking. I made a pad for the inside out of some old velveteen.

What I would like to do is now to take the Civil Service exam for the new assistants and go to the new National Gallery of Art in Washington, DC. I think I could pass. Of course that would take me away from Phil, but he is made of the kind of stuff that he will not ask me to marry him unless he can make the bulk of the money. And I refuse to hinder him in this. Three years may be a lot in our young lives. I like all his family too. It nearly killed me to leave Phil but is undoubtedly the best thing for the time being.

***

As I leave Ann Arbor, I sense there is a shift in my life. I've walked away from Phil, my one stable

Ready for life's changes

college beau. I feel strong enough to put distance between mother and me to begin making my own decisions.

***

June 1940—Washington DC

One semester of graduate studies at University of Michigan and I needed a break. It was time to pursue that feeling of really doing something. I thought of my college friend, Elizabeth Smith in Washington, D.C. She invited me to board with her and her mother for $20 a month at their home, 2153 California Street, as I looked for employment.

In August, fate intervened and my life radically changed. Betty invited her co-worker, Keith Adamson, home for dinner. I was leaving for a date to attend an organ recital at the Washington Cathedral, but Keith waited until I came home to ask me to dinner at his fraternity house. He was quiet a looker. I never looked back. He swept me off my feet with attention, golf games on Haines Point, boat trips on the Potomac and stimulating conversation.

***

August 1940

Dearest Mama,

Keith is a student at George Washington University. Our social life is college parties, long conversations with international students about political life in Washington and the international affairs of their countries. Wow.

He works for the Federal Housing Administration and is Assistant to the Manager of the Radio and Motion Picture Division.

Working Girls in D.C.
Elaine on right

He is very interested in learning other languages. He learned Spanish practically on his own from Mexican farm workers in Kansas, where he's from. There is practically a rage for Spanish here since efforts of the Pan American Society have brought in lots of Spanish speaking people.

He finished two years at a small college in York, Nebraska, attended business school in Wichita and then went with a supply company in the oil fields in Seminole, Oklahoma. A friend of his convinced him there was more of a future in Washington where he could work and finish college at the same time. So he came.

Mama, we feel we are very much alike, especially in our responses. I know I lack what he gained in working five years. How's that for a good start? We've begun to hear wedding bells.

***

Jan 20, 1941

Dear Mama,

I answered an advertisement for a primary teacher's assistant, at the Whitehall Country School in Bethesda (ritzy, very private). I was asked instead to help out in the kindergarten department, as the other position had been filled. Small salary.

I am gaining enough experience to let me know whether I want to continue in the kindergarten field. I think the answer is no. I can be patient for two weeks but longer than that is hard on the nerves, especially with about 10 little ones. I never knew there were so many "rubbers" (galoshes) in the world, or that you can be stepped on, kicked, and annoyed in so many ways. I applied for a couple of other positions that didn't materialize.

Remember I love you. R

***

February 2, 1941

Dear Mama,

I've thought for a long time, how I should tell you when the time came that I love Keith enough to marry him. To live on the little he makes and to work to make him happy with his work, his life and us. We won't have very much at first but Keith is steady at his job, well liked and capable—he has the most wonderful blond hair. Never before have I ever wanted to work so closely with someone. There are lots of things I'm plenty nervous about. Such as, what you will think of him and the ins and outs of marriage.

But he's loveable for his sweetness and his plain common sense and his love of truth, a home with all the things that go with it, children and grandparents and trouble. Before I wrote this letter I was afraid, but now somehow I feel like you're in on it and that makes things swell.

Anyhow I never knew things could feel so good inside. I'm close to him like I never was to anybody else. And I think you will like him too. News and stuff later –

Love, Elaine

***

April 17, 1941

Dear Mama,

My days have been full of long hours thinking about every phase of married life. So for better or worse I feel prompted to go ahead and take what life has to offer him. Not without a feeling of reticence, and fear, or apprehension in view of our past family experiences, but still open to a change of point of view.

Keith is more extroverted than introverted in his dealings with people. He will take me out of my excessive pensiveness and into a more 'southern' mode of living. We talked about how we feel we were both born to bloom in the neutral life of the south and to wither up and die in the social life of the north.

I would not have a child right away. I've learned a year of married life is much more advisable for congeniality—chance being taken into consideration.

I have been thinking seriously about when to get married, etc. Considering the draft first, only because it is imminent and also considering that Keith has been cooling his ardor and his heels since Jan 1, when he wanted to go to Maryland and elope.

***

May 15, 1941—Wedding Plans

Dear Mama,

I want to wear a real wedding dress to tell my children about, and a beautiful wedding veil. No matter how simple the wedding I can dress as bride. I want a long dress in white or pale pink organdie with ruffles and embroidery— made by yours truly; a short veil and a small bouquet. Keith can wear a dark suit.

I have the diamonds Gramma gave me for my wedding ring. Keith can decide how to use them to make it as simple as he wants. I remember they came from the ring Grampa gave Gramma as Aunt Georgie's birth gift. You said Gramma received the Music Box when you were born.

Elizabeth could be my maid. I want Uncle Doc and Aunt Ella and all the rest of them if they could come. I would miss them so much if they couldn't.

Keith's mother will no doubt come alone. Yes, you will want to come early to help me with the eternity of stuff to be handled. I got started seriously today for the first time and am frightened, first

Mr. & Mrs. Keith Adamson

by the prospect of Marriage (with a capital M) and second by everything that has to be done in such a hurry. I have to order calling cards and wedding announcements—no invitations, I think. All invites by telephone or letters. Food for the reception, license, flowers for church (I wish daises came out earlier).

Let's see on expenses: License -$2.00, Minister -$5.00, Pajamas - $5.95, Shoes -$1.00, Shoes -$5.00, Food -$10.00, Announcements -$15.00, Flowers -$20.00. [Servants- $10.00 – Gloria's mother-in-law wants to help do this.] Rough total, $120.00.

Let me know if you can come end of next week and stay that week, or if you can come sooner. I need you desperately.

Love, Rowena

***

June 6, 1941- Our Wedding Day

Our wedding was at five-thirty in the afternoon. The day was perfect, cool with a brilliant sun. The church decorated with two large baskets of white gladioli at the sides, and my favorite, baskets of white daisies on the altar.

So excited as I dressed in the floor length dress I'd made. It had a square neck and fitted bodice with a full skirt and three-inch ruffle at the bottom. My veil stood up in a shirred puff of that same material. In the front it fell over my face as I walked toward Keith and in the back it was a little longer than my skirt. I carried a little round bouquet of small white rosebuds and baby's breath. I wore Mama's filigreed pearl necklace for something borrowed and for my something blue, Elizabeth's engagement ring, a blue sapphire. Keith slipped a simple band on my finger inset with Gramma's diamonds.

Two hundred guests, friends and acquaintances attended. There was no reception but we received our guests in the vestibule of All Souls Episcopal Church. Then we went downstairs for the photographer. As we left, friends showered us with rice.

We planned to go to Elizabeth's just to change, but a few friends surprised us there with a nice wedding cake and fruit punch. After an hour or so we were anxious to get on our way, unaware Keith's frat brothers had taken our luggage. We only got as far as the Lafayette Hotel in DC.

***

This poem oozed from every pore as I realized how much I loved Keith.

132

Holy Matrimony
The beauty that I saw in the mirror
Was the woman that I had hoped to be all my life.
The change from "the me" I had known,
was almost more than my heart could stand.
This was what true "holy matrimony meant!
Nothing in this world could even match such beauty.
No wonder 'matrimony' could be known as 'holy'!
I was wholly his, and he was totally mine—
He had been totally mine, and I was wholly his.

***

October 22, 1941— Married Life

Dear Mama,

You sho' would be surprised at your baby if you could see her this morning. She's been working for two and a half days at the Riverside Stadium taking care of the switchboard and doing typing on the side. I get $19 a week, which is good for not doing much work from nine to five. But in the evening I can hardly make it to my class on time. Soon though I am going to run out of cans and be desperate to go to the grocery store. We are eating a lot of Scrabble —$8 a week food budget.

The day after you left, Keith happened to go to the State Department to deliver some film from FHA to their film division. They got so interested in him and his Spanish ability they sounded anxious to have him come over there and work. That office is the Cultural Relations of the State Department. Of course he has to go through the rigmarole of papers and everything. They really were very interested in him. Hope, hope, hope. Salary $2000, which is $170 a month.

Saturday night we had a small party. I candied some apples with molasses and boy were they tough. We had a regular laughing riot. I laughed so hard I wet my pants. There's a little new pressure on my bladder these days.

I feel fine. I don't lean over so well and sometimes Keith has to fix my shoes, but it isn't really incapacitating. And my appetite is excellent. Even working I haven't gotten very tired. I am bigger, which goes without saying, although they don't seem to have noticed it here.

Rowena

Dec 7, 1941—War Declared

Our radio blared this evening as we heard President Roosevelt,—*A day that will live in infamy - Pearl Harbor, December 7, 1941. The attack on the United States Naval Base at Pearl Harbor, Hawaii, commenced at 7:48 am Hawaiian time, conducted by the Imperial Japanese Navy.*

The US declared war on Japan Now we are in another war. Keith anticipated being sent to Europe and this leaves us up in the air but doubles the worry we feel about Keith being conscripted. He is in the prime age group of the men to be sent to the front lines sooner than later.

***

February 27, 1942

Telegram to Rowena N. Pennock

DAUGHTER-APRIL-ROWENA-LACOSTE-ADA-MOSN-BORN-COLUMBIA WOMEN'S HOSPITAL.

Keith

***

In the days that followed I told Mama that motherhood was bringing new challenges for me. Growing up with no siblings, I had never been around babies or tended to their needs. Most of my life I'd only been concerned with my own needs.

***

September 1942

Dear Mama,

Keith is studying hard and works full time to support us. I'm learning to care for and be with an infant full time. This is a new world for me. Fortunately, Beedee lives close and loves to take April to her house often. She even has a crib and toys for her. What a help she is to this inexperienced young mother, newly pregnant again. I told you this new event is coming in the spring, haven't I? Rowena

***

May 1943

The war is swirling around us. As university students it is the highest topic of conversation. Also living in Washington puts each battle in Europe or the Pacific or Congressional decision top news of the day.

Keith graduates from George Washington University. Our second daughter, Linda Lee Fermor Adamson, was born on May 19. My stay at Colombia Women's Hospital lasted almost up to graduation day.

***

Dear Mama,

I imagine Keith has done well in his final exams. He doesn't rattle on like I do but from the little he says I know all will be well. I will be home from the hospital in time to attend the ceremony at Constitution Hall.

Beedee offered to watch the babies for us. Dulasky from the office gave us their bassinette. Mrs. Adamson bought a blanket for Linda. Beedee is eternally buying things for April. I have been reading Bernadette and must stop.

Lots of Love, Rowena

***

November 13, 1943

Telegram to Mrs. Rowena Pennock—11:00 AM

WAS SWORN IN TODAY AS ENSIGN AM TO REPORT AT NAVY OR WORK NEXT WEDNESDAY NO NEWS YET ABOUT ANY TRAVEL AM VERY DELIGHTED OF COURSE WOULD YOU BE WILLING TO MOVE GOODS FROM DETROIT TO SEDWICK LOVE – KEITH AND ROWENA

***

In early 1944 Keith was sent to Norfolk for training. He suggested I take the girls to Sedgwick where his family could care for us if he shipped out.

I decided eventually to take the girls but it was difficult to leave them there. I was expecting another baby and due to our financial situation I needed to give birth at a military hospital. I returned to Norfolk. Grammy Adamson wrote that both girls had measles but were recovering.

In 1945 our son, Marque Keith Adamson, was born in Norfolk. The announcement was clever:

Ensign Adamson with family, Elaine, April, and Linda

135

The launching of the "Tender" USS Marque Keith Adamson at
N.O.B. Baby Yards, Norfolk, Va.
0145 May 7, 1945
Dockmaster: Dr. Milton M Rozan
Displacement: 6 lbs., 8 oz.
Sponsors: Keith and Rowena Adamson

Keith was on a train to San Francisco to join the 7th Fleet and duty in the Philippines when he got news via the Red Cross. My telegram to Mama said, COME IMMEDIATELY.

Most of Keith's duties in the Philippines, the two years he was there, were in a training capacity due to his fluency in Spanish. The Victory ribbon he was awarded included one for American Theatre, Asiatic-Pacific-Philippine-Liberation.

***

Difficulties in the marriage, three kids, no help. Very stressful.

November—1945

Dear Mother,

You must know from experience that the reason I have not been writing is that I have been worried, and worried, and worried, about all the problems of this household. I am having a hell of a time sticking it out. . . . and to think of some way of adjusting to this marriage. All of my thoughts come to nothing.

I wrote Keith I could not go on as we did before, as much as I did not want to hurt his feelings. His answer was that he was glad I brought the subject up because he felt that way also.

From there I have not progressed very far. Keith's attitude is that our troubles have basically been due to material setbacks, and our relationship, and I am only too aware of the fact that we do not love each other. I have spent five years trying.

There is always the possibility that when he returns we can work out our difficulties satisfactorily, but my heart has taken such a wicked beating, I don't know if I can take a corpse and do anything with it.

When I think I have another five months of insanity before I can make any decisions about us, when for five years I have wondered how and what to do, I just don't feel like I have the courage...How can they know the desperate sense of loss I feel. Whatever virtues I might have had are so terribly tarnished I feel I've lost all touch with honesty and integrity. There must be a better life somewhere.

Love, Rowena

***

Sedgwick, 1946

At Keith's parents farm, I got to know Grampa Adamson. I liked him so much I wrote a poem about his kindness. Only Grammy had been at our wedding five years years before.

Another Generation
I never knew him when
He wasn't kind to everyone.
I never knew him when
He wasn't gracious to Grandma.
I never knew him when
He wasn't good to all of us.
I never saw him when
He wasn't quiet, 'round the bull.'
I never knew him, when
He wasn't jolly, 'mongst the chicks'.
I never saw him show
Impatience, with the 'little ones'.
I never found distrust
Of any relatives or friends
I never felt distrust
When I presumed to cut his hair.
I never knew him to
'talk short' to anyone…ever.
I never knew him not
To be asleep in the rocker…
When all of us would come home.
"OH!?"…"you all home already?"
One day God claimed him for
Himself…cause He…loved Grampa.

***

I enjoyed writing for the local paper, the *Sedgwick Panagraph*. I gave them an article every week although we discontinued my by-line. The Dept. of State doesn't allow its families to write under name.

One week my article was on the atom bomb test, next on the German Battleship Prinz Eugen, a great prize of American victory in the war. Then I did an article on the evacuation of Bikini Island.

I wrote letters to Keith on our various expenses and a budget, which was a joke. The money was just going out, that's all. At least it is going for something permanent, a new home.

Finally I heard he was in San Francisco, California, separating from the Navy on April 16, 1946. He came through Sedgwick to see his family and be with us. When Keith returned from his tour in the Pacific, he stepped back into the job waiting for him at the State Department.

***

1946 – New House — Falls Church Virginia

Dearest Mother,

I know I never write enough and yet have so many things to talk over with you. Naturally, trying to keep up with our long distance house building has got me stewing.

It's small, second small bedroom, one bath and small kitchen. Grounds are wooded. It's on a hillcrest, no sidewalk, blacktop street, ½ mile to stores in Falls Church.

Monthly cost is $60, telephone $4.75. But, oh, the other expenses – well it's a home; something we haven't had together, but small for a family of five.

***

June 1946

Dear Mama,

Do you plan to go to Detroit to sort the furniture you and Joe divided and left there four years ago? Keith and I are both so thrilled over the piano, I hope you do not regret saying we could have it. The large sofa, the sewing table, my rug, mirror, deep chair and the secretary desk should make us a super living room.

Say, why couldn't I meet you in Detroit for a day when I am on my way back from Kansas and you are there to sort the furniture. Can we jiggle our dates to match? We expect to go into our house July 1 or before.

Rowena

***

Fall 1946—225 Monroe Street, Greenway Downs, Falls Church, Virginia

Dear Mother,

From what I have seen so far, April has been playing with the typewriter again. She may be a writer someday. She started nursery school last Monday, and has not mentioned much about what happened.

We moved into the house when there was no electricity, gas, or anything except water. For the first day they gave us a long extension cord to the next house, for my hot plate. I have two pulley lines to hang clothes on. All three hovering over me now, because I should be fixing their dinner. Yes, I am a mother of three small children trying to make this place a home,

I did not realize the added burden of school for April. Now it is a question of getting all of them ready each morning to take her, everyday going and coming seven miles to school.

Honestly you would pop if you had to be with small children all the time. I am about to collapse tonight, and I am used to it. Keith comes home so late these days. I am glad he is home on Saturdays and we can either do things here or I can do a little shopping. I even had my hair done twice.

***

Feb 10, 1947

Dear Mother,

April is almost five. Party? Got the big package today with those beautiful down quilts. Gosh I forgot how nice they are. The girls are wearing the blue berets you sent. I am so pleased over the extra dishtowels too.

Keith is a teaching fellow at George Washington University, has an eight o'clock class in beginning Spanish. Lately he has been doing a couple of hours every night at the library. He finally finished the budget at State. It is mimeographed and ready for Congressional hearings.

Keith's fraternity shindig is March 20-21. ODK is national honorary leadership fraternity and I suspect some national figures will attend. Keith is GWU's official representative and president.

Having a lot of car trouble. It's so cold the water in the gas freezes on the carburetor points. Well below zero yesterday and today. Dinner is on the stove. So I will have to hustle. Lots of love, R

***

139

April 15, 1947

Mama,

I am taking all kinds of pills for one thing and another. I am three months pregnant, anemic again, with very low blood pressure, basal metabolic rate is minus 13. Have lost all of one eyebrow again. But I am expected to do all the same things as if I didn't deserve any better consideration. Love, R

***

October 20, 1947

Telegram to Mrs. Rowena N. Pennock, 11:53am

ERIC-EARL-SIX-POUNDS-TEN-OZ-BORN-12:02-EST-TO-DAY- COLUMBIA HOSPITAL ELAINE-FINE-LETTER-FOLLOWS—KEITH

Our fourth child, Eric, was a delight from the first giggle. Life in Falls Church was routine—fairly predictable, unpredictable, around babies and nursery school.

For relief, I love taking the children to interesting places in DC. The art galleries, museums, and historical sights all feed my insatiable appetite for learning and infuse me with energy.

Family Christmas, 1947

***

1949 — Overseas Duty

In the summer of 1949 Keith came home with the news he was to serve as Press Attaché at the American Embassy in Cairo, Egypt. His eager anticipation drove me to desperately seek help from Mama. She came and helped corral four little ones for multiple shots, and passport photos. Packing our household was our huge focus.

By September 16 we drove our new blue Chrysler sedan and assorted luggage to the Hotel McAlpin in New York. On September 20, settled in two cabins onboard the USS Excalibur, we sailed at 4:00 pm. It was hard to say our last goodbye.

On board, in one cabin, a mother washing diapers for an almost two year old, while keeping track of a three year old, a four year old and a six year old. A breather with a short stroll on deck, while the diapers

Family passport, 1949

and laundry dried hanging from upper bunks in my cabin, gave me a respite view of endless blue-ocean. In the other cabin, a father frantically studying Arabic or on deck socializing.

After an unforgettable week on the Atlantic Ocean we passed the cliffs of the Rock of Gibraltar and entered the Mediterranean. A few more days and we pulled into port at Marseilles, France with plans for a short visit in nearby Italy.

***

We crossed the Mediterranean from Naples for our port of call—Alexandria, Egypt. The day was terribly hot. Desert heat enveloped us. Whirling Dervishes crowded the dock performing their dances. Young boys dove into the water along side the ship. I was preoccupied keeping track of the children while I packed the last suitcases.

Finally we were all together on solid ground watching a huge crane off load our new shiny 4-door blue sedan. It safely took us over the desert road from Alexandria to Cairo, our new home. Miles of desert sand held a feeling of terror as well as excitement. We stopped at the single oasis and received a

Aboard USS Excalibur ready for an ocean voyage

warm Coca Cola in lieu of tainted water. The huge complex of the Giza pyramids loomed as we came toward Cairo. I was excited to imagine all the wonders we would see in the years to come.

***

Memories of Egypt —1950

I adapted to a diplomatic lifestyle when I realized my fluency in French launched me into exciting cross-cultural relationships. I felt I was an asset to my husband. I felt accepted. I had traveled overseas as a young girl. I felt I was finally on the inside looking out. Left behind were hours of caring for small children alone. Keith and I hosted international guests in our home. We sang together to entertain them as I played my baby grand piano. I enjoyed meals prepared for us by our house servants.

Archeology and ancient history pulled me into a new season of life. My interest in ancient things peaked during memorable visits to the Cairo Museum, as we climbed into the great pyramids of Giza, and later traveled to Jordan and Israel. My teaching

First Glimpse of the Pyramids

"gene" kicked in when I taught my children new languages and explored ancient treasurers in the desert with them. It included an attempt at early home schooling for April and Linda under the Calvert system from the University of Nebraska.

Being a diplomat's wife, home schooling mother, and adapter to foreign cultures finally overwhelmed "my cool." I placed our oldest daughter at the Cairo-American School in Maadi, where I had the opportunity to write an operetta for the students. Everyone participated in the exciting story of pioneers from Virginia and West Virginia, going to St. Louis to cross the Mississippi River and on to California. I felt excited to use my love of music and drama to write and direct it. I used my favorite songs from the American Folk Song Book. I made fifty 'Kansas-type' sunbonnets. Keith beat our toy drum for a marching beat.

An unexpected experience for my children took place on the back of a camel. The back end rose first, sending all four into their baby brother. Then the front raised and evened them out. They hesitantly overcame their initial fear of falling to the ground from its back

At the Cairo museum we were dazzled by thousands of incredible, centuries-old gold

Kids on camel

items excavated from Egyptian tombs. The children's eyes were round as saucers when they saw hair growing from mummies heads and their long fingernails.

***

I wrote about this place with words from my heart:
Cairo:
The first home abroad
Of the places we have lived,
I can give no comprehensive account,
No tour book type of guide that
Would interest the average stranger.

First photo was of a baby palm tree
In the front garden of the Embassy
At Cairo...the heat of the desert
Still in our hair and on our feet.

It was that very first day, we came,
Across the desert from Alexandria,
Along the way of the camels and sails
Following the canal and the desert road.

Our first hotel, near the Embassy
Was ours, on the fifth floor, looking
Down over a parking lot, and watching
A woman with a child across her shoulder.

Then, in Maadi, at a pension by the club,
Mme. Hochstein provided the four children
With enough bread and jelly for a lifetime,
And...a laundry roof to play games on.

The first home was a new built house
With angled steps up the front, angled
Both to the desert and the graveled road
Which led to the vibrant Nile, and Cairo.

From its balconies, we could see
The great pyramids, there being no house
As yet on that side; and "Moses" could see
Us, watching the place...where he was found.

This was 'Home', for three good years,
Grass and garden all around, with the Gists

In the house next door, and British people
Straight across the newly-graveled street.

As yet, there was no obstruction, so
The great pyramids assaulted us daily
With beauty, strength, and history...and...
The eternity of mystical science, all at once.

The flowing Nile, on the pyramids' side,
Was always alive with sailing 'feluccas',
With the comings and goings of Sudanese,
And constant commerce of dark, inner, Africa.

On that side too, was the western desert,
Sun broiling at midday, ballooning at
Sunset hour...and fleeting down when
That final second seemed...never...to come.

***

Cairo to Damascus—1951

On our visit to Jerusalem Keith and I stayed at the American Hostel. We "did" the city, on the Arab side. Because we were diplomats, assigned to the Arab country of Egypt, we did not feel free to travel in Jewish-controlled areas of the city.

In Bethlehem, we entered the church of the Holy Nativity through the donkey gate... Next we headed to the Sea of Galilee...and to the Gatenly Bridge to Jordan. At Aswan I lay down and took a short nap on the cool marble floor in the ladies room. At the border of Syria I rejected a strawberry drink. No Coke here, it was illegal.

When toward sunset we saw the walls of Damascus; we were ecstatic. There was a pool for diplomats we embassy women could use (we were in a Muslim country). This pool was almost in the middle of the river called Straight, in the middle of the city! We shopped along the street called "Straight", which St. Paul wrote about.

We enjoyed our time in Damascus visiting friends, without children, whom we left in Maadi with their Italian nanny, Valeria. We drove our rented car down to Beirut, going down and down around the hairpin curves. It was stunning to see the sea from our mountain departure, to arrive at last looking at the sun setting on the Mediterranean Sea.

***

Reassigned—1952
Noted in my journal:

Leaving Egypt was painful. There were many aspects of being a diplomat that gave me the freedom to investigate my interests without the necessity of daily care of the children. It had been a place that peeked my interests in areas of culture and history. I have a heart attachment to that country, and my heart will always be open to things Egyptian.

Keith tried to soften the blow by taking us to Paris, one of my other favorite places. The *real* ice cream milkshakes we enjoyed at the American Embassy café were a highlight we all remember. For three years, we drank globs of under-dissolved powered milk called KLIM.

We made a stop in London "to visit the Queen" and heard English spoken around us again. Those few days in Europe were a needed time of readjustment to western living.

A long, overnight TWA prop plane flight to New York brought us safely home. Renegotiating began for housing, schools and funds to pay for our growing children. Our row house at 2013 Klingle Road, NW, Washington, DC, was blocks away from the Washington Zoo. We heard nightly sounds of lion's roars and monkey chatter.

Keith was back at State and the children were in school— April 5th, Linda 4th, Marque 2nd and Eric Kindergarten. I'd been comfortable in DC many other times in my life, but this time I didn't fit.

To provide extra funds to ease our ongoing financial problems, I began selling a vitamin product called Nutrilite door-to-door. Compared to my life in Egypt I felt like I'd entered a time warp.

***

October 1954

Dear Mama,

Between July and October this year Keith spent days in New York… he went to Los Angeles, on TV or Radio every day. He interviewed the man who made the new Nutrilite training film. Small world.

Think we all could use North Carolina trip or beach sometime. Keith probably will not go with us.

***

November 1954

Keith is so happy these days he can even forget our money troubles. (Democrats elected) I wish he or I really knew how to manage.

Nov 30, 1954

Dearest Mama,

Keith wanted to go to Kansas for Christmas and now is almost decided it's too much money for us to spend. He made a true effort to take hold of the budget this time. But it remains to be seen how well he keeps up.

We've been involved in a lot of church activities at St. Albans. Bazaar projects, me in choir, Linda and April each in their own choir…and me teaching 4th grade Sunday School. Frankly I am too tired right now for my own good.

Keith is off on a Webelos Den meeting and planning a new set up around the tree for the electric train this Christmas.

I wish he felt like nightlife once in a while. I guess he really does, but holds it back the same as I do. LOL, R.

***

December 13, 1954

Dearest Mama,

Somehow, we all need you very badly this year. I know it is a chore to travel, but we sure want you to come.

For Christmas everybody needs a new shirt. The boys needed pants so bad Beedee bought them corduroys. They could use at least two more pairs each and the girls need blouses or sweater idea. April says she needs skirts. Linda already saved $44.95 and bought her own Christmas present, a bicycle! We had an old scooter fixed for the boys. I'm making Keith a dress vest for his birthday. And I've got to get at it! Merry Christmas, Rowena

***

Christmas 1954

Music calms me, especially Christmas carols. At this time of year my involvement in the choir fills my soul with pleasure as the familiar words roll off my tongue. In fourth grade I asked Mama if I could take a music class. Little did I know it would begin a life-long love relationship with Music. Piano lessons in high school showed my stepfather I was serious enough for him to purchase a baby grand piano for me. In college there were so many musical opportunities. I took advantage of as many as possible.

When the children were little, I sang them lullabies from operas and music I learned in college. I wonder if they remember this favorite of our? *Il est ne, le divin Enfant; Chantons tous son avenement!*

***

Spring 1955

Mama,

Our fortunes are always changing. For two weeks now Marque has had the mumps, a chore to keep him down. Now Eric has them. I'll have to sit on both of them or tie them to the bed. We anticipate the girls will have them also.

It's already hot here. We plan to take the first two weeks of August and stay a few days at Fontana Lake over in Tennessee Smokies. We all send love…R

***

June 1955—New Home

Dear Mother,

We found a house built in 1940. We offered $12,000 with $1,500 down. It is on a 150x150 lot and is well landscaped with nice front lawn. Our payments will be the same as the more expensive house we considered in Fairfax, but still need to ask you to loan us the down payment. We are anxious for you

Our dear yellow house

to see it. Surrounded by beautiful country and yet the closest to my work of anything we've seen.

Two miles from Chain Bridge on Langley Road, turn left on Merchant Lane, keep left until you reach the white cottage with Adamson on white post out front. Two miles to McLean, where children go to school by school bus each morning. Elementary and high school both new.

Elaine offered a position teaching English to foreigners at American University this summer at $100 per week.

Piano and your big table fit in living and dining of this house. Thank you Mom for helping us out with this project.

Love from all of us, Keith

November 1955

Dear Mama,

We've been more of what I'd call a real family in this little yellow house on Merchant Lane in McLean, Virginia. Perhaps it's because we have to work together to do needed repairs. It required the attic to be finished for the boy's bedroom. Keith stays home more. I think he likes living in the "country." One of the biggest hits we took was a hurricane. As it swept up the East coast, Keith, April and I, in pouring rain, dug a trench around the perimeter to apply black stuff to keep the basement from flooding.

If we are assigned overseas again, in order to afford it, I could teach at American University this summer. R

***

February 1956

I knew it couldn't be true. Just as we were comfortably settled in our little patch of heaven, Keith got orders for Ankara, Turkey. He went ahead. I stayed for the children to finish school. That left me, again, with all the packing, doctor's appointments, shots and trying to sell the house. I trusted myself to do this, but it's so difficult alone.

***

June 1956

Moving overseas has its exciting moments. I do well in a different culture, and I looked forward to having help in the house. Our wonderful houseboy, Hasan Kigusus from Romania, is a jewel. He and I understand one another in French. Nothing discussed, but emotionally in sync.

In Ankara the diplomatic circle is not as formal as Cairo, as it includes the US military. It is cosmopolitan, more western, of a new era, but we had to learn a new language. Thank goodness I was not expected to entertain on the same scale as Egypt.

Times had changed to make it acceptable for me, as a diplomat's wife, to have a job. I prepared last year at American University in DC to teach English at their campus extension program here. I feel fulfilled and on top of things. Teaching non-English speakers is what I truly enjoy. It can be so creative.

Our most exciting moment in Ankara so far was on a recent Sunday morning. I stood outside our pantry with my hands on two sides of the door frame. Suddenly my hands moved by themselves. One up and one down. My face indicated to Hasan I'd never experienced an earthquake. His first words were, *kosmak*, run. I did, only a matter of ten feet to the garden.

***

Istanbul 1957

Keith was promoted. Our lives changed, again. As a dutiful diplomat's wife I spent the summer packing our home in Ankara for the move to Istanbul. The train ride gave us the opportunity to view the Anatolian plain. Thankfully Hasan went with us.

Our one-complete-floor double apartment in *Bebek*, had a magnificent view of the Bosporus. We watched

oil tankers pass from the Black Sea to the Mediterranean. At night the lights from homes on the other side sparkled like magic on the water.

On the water's edge, near our apartment building, was *Rumeli*

Bebek, Istanbul Ottoman Tower

Hisar, an Ottoman era fortress and tower. Across the straits, on the Asiatic side, an identical tower, *Anadolu Hisari*, had been part of the city's defenses in 1452. A chain set between them and could be tightened to limit boat or enemy traffic.

***

Istanbul September 1957

Living in Istanbul, we faced a difficult schooling situation for April. Our decision for her future was made without much debate. We took a colleague's opinion for a boarding school in Switzerland. Now, when I think of an inexperienced fifteen-year-old girl, traveling from Istanbul to Geneva, Switzerland, on her own, with three train changes and an overnight stay alone in a major world city—was I crazy?

Even as April studied hard, the rules were confusing to follow. When she returned for Christmas vacation I felt she was unhappy being in a far away place.

***

Istanbul 1957

I missed the Shah of Iran's birthday party at the consulate last week. Letters of apology mailed.

I tried to get a hobby show organized to inspire this lethargic inhomogeneous American community to draw together. You see the big difficulty is that Americans among themselves feel the need for certain types of group activities to maintain their feelings of personal security... and at the same time provide American contact with those people of local importance in business.

I also write news items for the USIS newspaper.

I just had another idea: one of the English teachers here said she urges her students to go to the movies three times over so they catch the English and study it later.

***

April 15, 1958—Spring break

Dear Mama,

April's discontent with school in Switzerland is the reason for Keith's perpetual wakefulness. I can hardly get him to bed. It gets worse and worse. We asked the bank for more to send her back if that seemed the best course.

April says that she did not get any 'text' books until the end of December; that there is neither reference book nor library; that bread and water is the punishment for trivial infractions of something unnamed; in other words no education. (She liked the skiing.)

She and Keith are in Ankara to talk to the Air Force school there about her transferring for the rest of the year. It would help our budget and cause less worry. Rowena

***

April 28, 1958

Keith is trying to get the Turkish American University Association established. If we had 60 teachers of English we could use them all. For 200 places you will have 4000 applicants.

We are trying to get TAUA to sponsor a real University credit institute for the benefit of foreigners who want to study Turkish history and art, etc. in English.

We went to Turkey in early 1956, Keith was USIS Deputy Public Affairs Officer at Ankara. A year later he was promoted to USIS Public

Affairs Officer in Istanbul overseeing the country of Turkey. By the time I finished endless yards of curtains for our large apartment windows over looking the Bosporus, we were moving to the U.S. Army War College at Carlisle Barracks, Pa.

***

Summer 1958—Carlisle, Pennsylvania

By June we were on our way to Pennsylvania where Keith was selected to represent the State Department. He walked across the parade field for classes from our post housing. The children took a school bus into town. I relaxed with a wonderful new hobby, hooked rug making.

Spools of wool were left from the rug making factories nearby and I collected all I could afford to work the designs I drew. Keith and the boys joined me in finishing a few beautiful rugs.

I applied for copyrights on my rug designs. I hoped to see one produced with my hopscotch design. My creative juices make me happy.

***

When Keith and I are "on the same page," I feel on top of my world. But this relationship I have with him isn't calculated to make a female body feel relaxed. He stirs up my emotions and then just leaves me. Not that this is any different than it was before. It's just that my hope for improvement is slowly being killed off.

For my birthday he took me to New York for a special event. He met with Henry Cabot Lodge and the Israeli Ambassador. The second night we had dinner with friends from Istanbul, and Joe Haff of the New York Times and Dolunay, former director of the Hittite Museum we had met in Ankara.

***

July 1959—5823 Old Chesterbrook Road, McLean, Virginia

After Keith's graduation at Carlisle he returned to his position with the United States Information Agency. We were back living in McLean, same town, different house. Nice to know the neighborhood.

I began to work on my Master's degree in Linguistics and TEFL, (teaching English as a Foreign Language) at American University (courtesy of a Ford Foundation grant).

***

June 1960

I did it. A year later I finished my degree. That summer I taught at their Language Center and worked part time at the Center for Applied Linguistics. I knew my subject and enjoyed being part of a group who also loved to encourage non-English speakers.

The Graduate

***

Summer—1961

A great year, but big changes in our family. Keith is assigned as Public Affairs Officer for the country of Colombia, South America, in Bogota. Fulfilling opportunities at American University for me were exchanged for packing boxes and worry about my daughters left behind. We are on our way overseas again with the boys. As they say, *Hasta la vista.*

***

Bogota, Colombia-Living at 9,000 feet—1961

• I attended the dedication of the *Esquela Rowena Adamson* after an arduous trip to a mountain village. I was surprised and honored to have a small school named after me. After all my years in education, my name was over the door.

• We didn't have enough money to cover our daughter's schooling in the US and entertain properly here. What an awful worry. I taught English as a Second Language at the Jesuit University for funds to offset our needs.

• My son, Marque, ever the surprise, came home from school over the back fence of our garden. The sentry for the Papal Nuncio next door sent a young soldier to tell me we might have a thief. I assured him the man in question was my son.

• Keith dropped the beautiful gold ring with an engraved carnelian signet stone I had made for him. The stone shattered. I kept the gold.

- In a terrible rainstorm, the house seemed to 'bend' with the wind and rain. The basket-like weave of the roof resisted the fury of the storm.

- We grew our own lettuce and tomatoes in a nice twenty by fifty foot garden. The sun was equatorial and made everything respond. We always had the makings of a salad.

- A few orchids hung in baskets along the sides of the porch roof near the small terrace that led into the living room.

***

March 1963

Our tour was cut short in March when Keith was recalled to Washington to be interim director of the Voice Of America. He'd had on-the-ground experience with the Voice in our overseas embassies. By September, Congress had appointed John Chancellor as the Director and Keith returned to USIA at State.

The boys and I followed in May, at the end of school. After the wifely duties of packing, and drying tears, there was the heartache of missing one last tour in a gold mine. When we landed in Miami, the boys and I took a $99 Greyhound Bus for a stop-n-go tour across the USA. We visited historical places, ate road food and stopped for good visits with relatives in Kansas and New Orleans. We continued to a new home, again in McLean.

***

Time for re-evaluation

My life is running on two main tracks—family needs and personal interests. The constant flips and changes kept me tired—tired of readjusting. Frequent moves brought additional people into my life, people I wanted to keep in touch with, but the efforts put more responsibilities on my plate.

My daughters are on their own now. I still juggle the boy's needs, with Keith's career, entertaining, hobbies, and education. I love learning, which fills deep pockets in my life. But my greatest desires are for affection, relief from worry and enough money.

I feel split into thousands of pieces until I am giving so little energy to each. I am losing myself. I am losing Keith.

McLean, Virginia—December 1965

This past year I chased linguistic rainbows in three counties, taught teachers the new linguistic English grammar and dreamed of a new book each week—one to read or one to write. Good all around.

I constantly worked on designing a language project or learning game. I made plans to sell a game, saw someone about a job or an educational program. I think this counts as being fractured. How do I stop and smell the roses?

***

McLean, Virginia 1966

This year Keith had to go back and finish things in Bogota. He is also studying Vietnamese for possible change of orders. He has amazing language abilities in Spanish, Arabic, Turkish, so-so French, a little Russian and now Vietnamese.

I get by with Spanish, a "tiny taste" of Arabic, some Turkish and good French. As I've studied the basics of linguistics it has taught me ways to look at the foundations of languages. Very helpful and interesting.

I have a few possibilities for a teaching job. This gives me hope. If I could only focus on the Grammar Games project and get it sold. I need a trademark. Maybe it could be: Taggme, A Grammar Game.

We badly need the little money I earn. So I commute from McLean to Leesburg to teach English, but my checks are not timely and I need to be paid for travel. It's always about money. I remember writing my mother before we were married. I would stand by Keith "to live on the little he makes and work to make him happy with his work, his life and us." It's hard to keep that vow with the financial pressures we have. Moving every few years only adds to our debts. Can't get a handle on budget or prices.

***

September 1966

Keith's mind is already "over there somewhere." It always leaves first as he imagines the possibilities of a new country assignment and the problems to solve there. At a far eastern restaurant, I ate a strange meal for the last time with my husband. I could not understand his preoccupation with everything "Oriental." Before we left the restaurant he was already a stranger. I do not think I ever saw him again. He left for Vietnam.

154

February 1969

Dear Journal,

My world fell apart. All the men I've loved have abandoned me—my father, my stepfather, and now my husband. His recent letter from Reno, to establish residence he said, in order to file for divorce, was so cold it's as though he'd never known me. It hurts like fire. I love him with all my heart. Was I not paying attention? Probably. With all the focus on my other interests and his travels, we grew apart.

***

April 1969

Mama,

Got letter from Keith's lawyer that didn't say much constructive. Have to do my part of the income tax.

When I try to study, I think of Keith and get wound up. The only answer is work and pursuing the objectives of my dissertation. I still need to learn the French morphology and phonology. I have reviewed all the French grammar in three books. Still one more because the proficiency exam comes first.

***

To keep from becoming immobile I am pouring myself into classes at Georgetown University for this Ph.D. in Linguistics. Possibly my mind will replace my broken heart if I stay strong and study diligently. I am nearly paralyzed with the mental and physical fatigue of preparing for exams.

Lots of Love, R

***

April 5, 1970—A Prayer

I cannot face my faults, Oh, Lord,
I cannot face mistakes I made;
I know I am a fool;
Yet, Thou who property it is
Always to have mercy, Oh, Please,
Please lead me through the water's cool;
Wash off the layers of my pride,
Clean out the craven, contrite heart,
And purify 'my wool';

155

The tapestry I weave today
Of theory and fact and word
Translates my trepid soul;
Designs must hold and constant stay,
The forms of 'be' and 'do' take shape;
I must not will to fail.

***

June 3, 1970

There are times in a person's life when they lose direction and have to regroup to find out where they are going. That is my situation right now.

***

October 9, 1970

I've shut myself off from feelings. When I think of this situation in a hateful way, I feel my life, my strength and all the love I wish for myself being prostituted. I simply must get on with the next step in life.

***

October 28, 1970

Dear Mama,

Mme Mikus told me that my work showed so much emotional strain it was recommended I wait until spring to take the oral examinations. The problem is not so bad in my French, as language, but I really am not thinking straight.

It is probably better for me to look away from the stink around the divorce. It only bottles up whatever creative energy I have and stifles my soul. And I don't 'feel' divorced. I keep resenting being put in this ambiguous position.

I think the ugly atmosphere in Washington reflects the deception and the enormous farce going on in Vietnam.

Lots of love, R

***

November 2, 1970

"...went to the lawyer's Friday to sign that I had not been receiving support."

March 25, 1971

Dearest Mama,

Yes, I could use a new typewriter...someone got a fine long-carriage electric Royal in good condition for $80 at the government auction.

Have new class at Blair beginning Monday night...that will mean seven hours of teaching Mon and Wed for a month.

Much love, and thanks for all the loving support, Elaine

***

April 24, Saturday 1971

Dearest Mama,

Wednesday I got a call from the International Reading Association in Atlantic City requesting me to come and bring a presentation of my Grammar Games mobiles. The audience was unconditionally convinced of its applications and several people bought one on the spot.

Wow. People were interested in my Grammar Game – very encouraging.

I got some sea air and loved it.

***

June 30, 1971

Dear Mama,

I have seven hours of teaching a day. I got a new version of the Grammar Games worked up. And I have the copyright up to date, as the Golden Books man said... and the trademark is "Trust in Print"... a Trust in Print by Linguistics Research Associates.

To bed. Lots of love, Elaine

***

I am trying to hard to support myself teaching or designing new materials for ESL classes. My days are filled with working on my Ph.D. classes and my Phonemic Dictionary of English for the dissertation.

I'm trying to sell teaching materials I've copyrighted and have resorted to boarding an international student from Greece. I'm helping him get his green card to finish his school, as well as help him get customers for his home business.

This presents a difficult living situation for me, full of tension. I am restricted to my home to help run his business and must also be available to teach my classes in the evening for my income.

August 7, 1971

Dear Mama,

They are having a workshop in Montgomery Country for the leaders of the TOFEL people, and they have asked me to come and give a demonstration on the development and use of visual aids in that field.

***

November 17, 1971

Dear Mama,

One of my private English students passed her Americanization test today. All thrilled.

I have an application in to the National Endowment for the Humanities for the phonemic dictionary. I believe I have a good chance to get it.

Lots of love, R/Elaine

***

January 15, 1972

Dear Mama,

You have told me many times that discipline is a good thing. Well, I just have to discipline you. My great fault is not having done it sooner. Time and again, your 'discipline' cost me anguish. Now the time had to come to stand up to you for my son Marque and your treatment of him.

There is a letter you kept for many years, the one where I asked for my freedom when I was 24 and married. I needed the exercise of growing up. But you were unwilling to leave off dominating. I let you get away with terrible things against my children and me…and Keith, I suppose.

But you insisted on never saying you were sorry; never admitting that you could be wrong, never let anyone have any authority of their own. As a result, my children learned that they could not trust me to stand up for their rights. Only, this time, I am.

Even if Keith was weak, and even if we had broken apart for other reasons, this business of a backhanded slap is simply dishonesty in another form.

People are more important than the gifts you give them. People who know me have been hoping that someday I would stand up for my rights as a person. Adult shouldn't have to beg for their emotional freedom. I should be able to obey you and love you without being penalized for it.

People should obey you because they love you, not because you demand it.

One of the reasons, I never admitted to myself, for marrying at all was to have someone who would help me keep you at a distance. This is a terrible admission, whether to myself or to you.

I couldn't have the strength to say all this to you if I didn't have some recent counseling myself. My love for you is based on the thousands of acts of kindness and sacrifice you have willingly made and done for me.

Instead of working in a high school somewhere to help them, I was willing to let you carry the financial burden for us, and you were willing to carry it in order to have dominion over me, as always.

Honest caring should be our New Year motto.

***

1980— Georgetown University

Dear Dr. Alatis,

I would like to send Georgetown University the work I have done. The Phonemic Dictionary may be an inspiration to those who study in the library.

My theory of the 'Grammar Game' was most successful in class the years I taught at the University of Virginia in Arlington. Also the year I taught the teachers at Leesburg High School. Its application has been a joy.

Thank you, Rowena Adamson

***

In 1985 I moved to New Orleans to care for my mother. First we lived in a small apartment on Marengo Street not far from her church. I brought what I could pack in my car, sent a few boxes by UPS and left what possessions and little stability I had behind.

I had been "nominated," actually, the only one who could go to her and stay. Mama was a pretty feisty lady into her late eighties now. She had sustained some physical injuries in a purse snatching and then a fender bender. She needed my help. It would be sixteen years before I was alone again.

Rowena & Elaine

I enjoyed being a part of the vibe here. I found a part time teaching position at University of New Orleans. Memories of

Mardi Gras were relived in parties we were invited to attend. Mama said travel made her feel alive and we visited relatives or toured parts of the city. It relieved me of her incessant demands at home.

***

May 31, 1988

Dear Children,

The trip was fabulous. On arrival at Hawaii, greeted by Linda's shining face and Eleanor beaming one too, we found ourselves beautified by great flower leis...first we have ever had. We were so pleased all during the visit to see the variety of people and variety of flowers they wore.

Mama got used to their dog. Eleanor got used to us. We always had

good food. You may not realize this was my birthday gift...seventy years. We went to the impressive Arizona Memorial, and the odorous Dole Pineapple plant downtown.

The extension of Waikiki drive is a beautiful road that climbs the cliff of Diamond Head and gives a view out over the surfers who try their luck. Linda drove us all the way up to Waianae on the north shore and then around to Waimanalo to see the dolphins at Sea Life Park. Our last stop was at Hanama Bay where Mama got 'baptized' in the Pacific. She is ninety-five you know. Her feet sank in the wet sand and down she went, her face covered for a few seconds. Linda and I helped her to a log near the water where she said, "I thought I was fish bait!" The lifeguards loved that line.

Love, Mom

***

February 1, 1990

Dearest my little ones all,

Mama came to the table this morning saying, 'we are so lucky.' And we are. She can still take her nighttime bath, make the bathroom by herself and shut and open the car door when the spirit moves her. But she believes she can't walk across open ground without me beside her. Nor can she tolerate being alone for very long. She screamed at me yesterday, "I don't want to die alone, I'm going with you."

Otherwise our lives depend on the TV, newspapers and repairman. We think and talk of you and your interests all the time.

Lots of love, hugs, kisses, and prayers, Mother

***

Rummage sale at church

Looked in the basement for things to bring. Found my bean shooter used in 1924. And my 'Mammy Doll', kept all these years. Black, she is, and homemade.

I hope you all think of me a little, and more or less kindly. I adore you all from the first to the last person and from the first to the last hours of the day.

I want to sign one of those living wills, which says I don't want to be kept alive on machines.

Love and kisses, Mother

***

January 4, 1993

We buried Mama today at Lake Lawn Cemetery in Metairie. I tried my best to care for her until her death. A new place was made for her box beside her father and mother in the H.L. Nick plot. April, Eric and I stood under the graveside canopy as our minister Mark Gasque read the burial service.

She'd fallen at home and was in a coma the month of December. Christmas in a hospital was a new experience as I spent her last days and night in her hospital room, 3rd floor, Southern exposure at Turo Baptist Hospital, New Orleans. I prearranged her burial but was not emotionally ready for her to leave me. We had shared seventy-six years on this planet.

Two months later my son-in-law died of a massive heart attack. I flew to Maryland to be with my daughter, April, now a young widow. I think we all were in shock processing two deaths in the family in such a short time. Grief never ends, it can fade at times.

***

November 15, 1997—My 80th birthday

My family honored me today at a lovely dinner in Front Royal, Virginia, arranged by my son, Eric and his wife, Linda. Each of my children brought a grandchild or two to be part of our time together. We shared stories of other times and licked our lips at the tasty dishes and wine served. Lovely pictures remind me of that special time and how I love my children. I wore the special Egyptian gold necklace made by my friend Onig of Cairo. I felt like a princess.

***

November 27, 1994

Dear Grandaughter Carolyn,

I have wanted to tell you about my dictionary. It has been the delight and burden of my heart for many years. In 1971, I wrote a plan for it. By 1975, I was inspired by someone who confirmed my ideas could be computerized. In 1980 I got serious; I finished the dictionary. It is "my baby." I can't stop talking about it. It never seems to be really done to my satisfaction. It is finally going to be printed.

All I want—anytime, Christmas or whenever, is appreciation of my work.

Love, Gramma

PS - I believe language is the "Mine of the mind."

***

April 9, 2000 Hermit Basin, Colorado

Dear Father of us all,

My first thought is to ask forgiveness for my faults, so many prompted by ego and self-indulgence. Let the clear water of your Spirit clean my soul. Take away the fears that crowd my day.

Protect and guide my children, keeping them under your care...lead them to You as to the great "Continental Divide" between good and evil.

As for me and my life's work, I lay it all at your feet. You know better than I do how to use this for the betterment of other people. Help me make clear that the structure of sound is your doing, although implemented by mankind to show your inventive mind.

In all humility, Rowena Elaine

***

2005

The mountains of Colorado came alive in my poetry. There is so much beauty around me as I share my daughter's home nestled in pine trees on a mountain road. My books surround me. I can read, write, and enjoy a walk with a neighbor, or my sweet granddaughter and her dog. I like it here. My daughter's friends come to visit and we go to a Victorian tearoom in town.

April and I had a trip to Washington DC this year. It was my first experience on the new Metro. What a difference from the old days and the traffic. Many memories were brought to the surface as I remembered

being a new bride, a new mother and a diplomat's wife here. By my rough calculations I believe I lived in DC 20+ years.

Granddaughter Carolyn, Linda, April, & Mom

2007

Dear Journal,

I am aware of a recent trip April and I took. The airplane ride was nice and we landed right in Lafayette, Louisiana. As we looked around the town I remembered many places where I once lived as a child. I later visited my father there in the summers. We had a nice visit with my cousin, Orey LaCoste and his wife, Judith. Hard to believe he and I have lived this long. April and I visited the cemetery at St. John's where my father and many of my LaCoste family are buried.

***

2008-2012

Dear Journal,

I sense undercurrents of judgment and criticism—of me, my mind, my beliefs. I am in a fog, lost on the path I chose; of education, teaching, music and family. I feel afraid. I know I am in a retirement community

I daydream about pleasurable memories of my childhood, my children. I had a small dog, a playhouse too. My daddy died. I remember my husband, Keith and my desperate wish to really know him. We had fun learning Spanish, Arabic, French, and Turkish together.

I have nightmares about my dictionary. Where is it? What will happen to it? My brain is still mine; my writings are still mine to correct or publish. What a vain hope.

My dreams of taking voice lessons at the Paris Opera. Just a dream it seems.

I think I was happy in the days as a young mother. I had to wake up early, dress the children, fix breakfast, find everyone's coats and books and maybe pack four lunches, and drive five or ten miles to one, or two schools, and maybe go another to be the teacher. I was needed

I had to pack our home to go to live overseas. Other memories fade in and out.

***

I live with a nice family now. A little cat lies on my lap. The lady who takes care of me gives me small chocolate Éclairs with my dinner. She doesn't let me have more than two. I feel safe and happy. Heaven is still waiting.

***

Remembering Our Mother

Mother had an innocent artist's heart. She loved color, music, and words. She loved flowers, especially gardenias and magnolia trees. She loved and could identify many gemstones. She surrounded herself with "antiques and soft things." She was usually ready to try new things. Her creativity was unstoppable. She made Egyptian dolls and designed and made hooked rugs. She wrote decent poetry and designed teaching tools and books for ESL. She had a facility with words. She knew proper English and taught us proper "I and Me" usage. She enjoyed reading classic literature and applying their principles to her way of thinking.

She was woken with "hot thoughts" in the early morning, she said. After age 80, she wrote hundreds of poems in the night. She heard the inner voice of God when it was quiet.

***

People who met her in her later years enjoyed hearing her many stories. She was friendly and happy. As she celebrated her ninetieth birthday, it was obvious she relished attention. Her twinkly eyes sparkled as she blew out a cake top

Rowena's hands on a book

of candles. She loved reading her book—the same one every day and a short walk into the fresh mountain air. Meals tailored for her health needs maintained her good energy. She flourished with caregivers who were diligent to her needs. It was their love and kindness, without many words, that infiltrated her soul and gave her peace in the six years before her death. She is remembered for a beautiful smile and sparkly eyes.

***

After a restless night and quick trip to the Emergency Room, Rowena's heart stopped on October 1, 2012. Her son, Eric, held her hand. She'd lived ninety-five years. She still had all her own teeth. She could read without glasses. She could hold a C# to complete a hymn in church.

***

Thoughts by her daughter April Adamson Holthaus

At a recent concert I heard the words Mother sang to us as children, in French or Spanish. Vivid memories brought tears. I felt sad she had not pursued her dream of a career in opera, but thankful we had benefited from her training.

I see part of her legacy in my life in my same love of beautiful things. That love transferred to caring about people. Her ideas and creativity never stopped. She wrote poetry, created meals from nothing almost without a recipe. She designed teaching materials because she cared for internationals. She challenged me to think. She loved learning and stayed on task, in spite of heartache, to complete her degrees. I'm proud to follow in her footsteps.

***

Thoughts by her daughter Linda Adamson

My legacy from mother gave me intellectual curiosity, the ability to energetically pursue ideas and cope with life's challenges. Her appreciation of art and music and nature continue in my own interests. In spite of her frequent depressions, anxieties, self-loathing and insecurities, she was also a person with opposite characteristics who would say, "Why?" and Why not?" and "Let's Go," and "Find out if you can!" I was able to pass many of these to my own daughter.

***

Thoughts from her son Marque Keith Adamson

Mother instilled in me a sense of wonder at all I see; a fascination with the art and creativity in every craft; an appreciation for the life that was preserved in all objects as the fruits of someone's mind and handiwork.

She taught me to love history and archeology and the sciences as the lifeblood of humanity; embodying the past, present and future of us all. Lastly was her love of others; perhaps as she aged she became less tolerant but she acted most of her life as a servant to them, teaching, helping, and encouraging them to seek knowledge and to better themselves.

***

Her son, Eric Earl Adamson, remembers

Mom and I shared a love of antiques, wine and languages, among other things. She was a great traveling partner on a Rotary speaking trip to Nice, France. I appreciated the confidence she always had for my pursuits and the pride she had in me for all I tried to accomplish. Her words of encouragement were always positive.

***

Thoughts from Barbara Rowzee, a Louisiana friend

Little did I know when I met April's mother and called her Row, it was the same name she'd been given in college. We felt comfortable together right away. We both loved thrift stores. During the next ten years, she told me stories of her life. She struggled with feelings of loneliness, rejection, and a sense she was unworthy. Her words sadden me. This women of great potential felt she had not achieved her personal goals.

As she grew older, she enjoyed talking about life in old New Orleans and her family history there. I'm so thankful to know she is at peace and enjoying eternity with her Savior Jesus Christ.

***

Mom's Caregivers—Thank You

The Liverett family and pets, and the Yerton family farm animals. Caretakers Valerie, Betty, Melanie, Jean and John who took loving care of Mom on a daily basis in two care homes for over four years. They became a vital part of her well-being during the last years of her life in Pagosa Springs. They loved her sweet smile and listened to funny stories of her life. She was an innate teacher. Our family is grateful to these dear people and the love they showed her and us.

My Heritage

April Rowena Lacoste Adamson Holthaus

April & Mother, Rowena Elaine

FAMILY CHART

April Rowena LaCoste Adamson, Smith, Holthaus
m. Michael O'Halloran Smith
m. June 1962—div. 1971
      Christopher Mark Smith
      Carolyn Elaine Smith
m. Hollis Lee Holthaus—b. June 9, 1936—d. March 13, 1993
m. April 30, 1971
      Andrea Leigh LaCoste Holthaus Sprague

CHAPTER SEVEN

*M*y heart is overflowing as I finish this book about the stories and histories of my family.

For the past twenty years I've read and re-read my ancestor's letters and journals. Details on the back of hundreds of photos, and on notes attached to personal memorabilia, helped bring them to life. Historical research helped me understand how their lives were impacted over the decades.

I found insights into their values of faithfulness, the reasons they highly regarded education and their dogged perseverance in the hard times. These honest letters slowly revealed their faith and how they remained steadfast in life's challenges and celebrated the good times. They inspired me to learn more about historical events that shaped their lives. I began to identify with them.

April

Historical research affords me insights to picture the struggles of their day. Searching court records, genealogical data, and maps of where they lived, brought into focus a truer picture around each woman's situation. I am the next generation in a long line of brave courageous women. I pray I pass these same lessons on to my daughters, granddaughters and great-granddaughters.

***

Three of my grandmothers were young widows, as was I. Two were divorced, as was I. One was deprived of her children for a time, as was I. Two lost a child, as have I. Their stories have ended except for the lessons they left us. After years of emotional investment in their words, I've begun to recognize their bravery and stamina in the face of similar trials in my life. Early events and lack of stability left me confused and heartbroken as I grew up.

***

When I was sixteen, I boarded a plane in Istanbul for school in Switzerland. My parents believed I was grown-up enough to handle life on my on. They gave me advice like: be a "good" girl, get a good education, be kind to people, and attend church when possible, but they left me without emotional and financial support. Though I felt grown-up and thought I could handle the world, I was really scared.

April at 17, 1959

I attended thirteen schools before I graduated high school. I lived in three different states in five different houses and in three foreign countries. Two years later I was a new Navy wife. Moving a few more times in two years, I had two babies and a husband at sea. My struggles reminded me of my mother's. I'd realized she needed practical help at times and I knew I did too.

In 1970, Someone came into my life and made all the difference in how I handled my life. I didn't, God did. Today I've grown to understand through His Word how much He loves me. His guidance gives me undeserved strength, mercy and wisdom to persevere through hard times I still experience.

***

My Mother, Rowena Elaine, taught me about overcoming difficulties in life—she kept going. Her love for her children seemed God-given. Her letters and her writings passed along a passion for words, music, travel, language and people. Time will allow her lessons to form their results in my life.

***

My grandmother Rowena's life overlapped my own for fifty years. We did not live close, but her stern influence was felt. I perceived her as the controlling force in our family. Writing her story helped me understand the choices she had to make. I saw how she coped after losing her father, and later, how she survived as a single mother in her late twenties. Education was her "mantra."

***

My great-grandmother, Almira, was a beautiful lady I'd admired in a large portrait. I knew her life was not easy but I didn't know her story. I began to understand Almira better as I read her letters. She was a woman of her times. She lived a life of relative ease in the late 1800's as a middle class mother and wife. She reacted to her husband's early death by feeling unable to face her future alone. Serious health issues and depression compounded her problems.

***

I knew my great, great-grandmother, Fannie Brown, only as an impersonal name on Ancestry.com. I began to picture her life in the context of Houma, Louisiana where she was born. I envisioned her as a little girl in 1848 on a sugar plantation. Then I found her signatures and those of her two husbands' in her memory book. Fannie became real.

***

I began the journey into the long ago past, to find my great, great, great grandmother, Frances Ann. She was a secret until I found a scrap of paper with the word, Houma. Court records listed her and her family in 1841 as residents of the parish. Other judicial records told of her stand against laws that disavowed women. I believe she was a strong woman who used difficult situations to give her strength then and to live through the Civil War.

***

"Letters provide us with a window into another world. They connect us with the past in a way that history books are unable, drawing us into another realm and revealing the nitty-gritty aspects of life. The researcher cherishes a collection of personal letters not just for historical facts recorded but for the private experiences uncovered. Through letters we are able to relieve a moment in time. It is as if we are touching history." *The Historic New Orleans Collection Quarterly, Vol XXVIL, Number 1—Winter 2010*

This quote resonates deep within me. Bayou Roots and its stories were written because I found letters in a moldy basement. I used them to connect me with my family's past in a way no history book ever could. Their signatures, letters, poems, and pictures formed each one into shadowy flesh-and-blood people I would recognize if I met them.

Knowing I have roots in the Louisiana Bayou gives me, an unsettled world traveler, a deep sense of finally belonging to a place and a people. I do have *Bayou Roots.*

ABOUT THE AUTHOR

APRIL ADAMSON HOLTHAUS grew up as the oldest daughter of an American diplomat. Her marriage to a Naval officer continued her travels and love for other cultures. Her worldview of people, places and the future has been impacted by travel and her faith.

She completed a Masters degree at Colorado Christian University three years after the death of her young husband and began a national newsletter for grieving widows. She also continued a home business in desktop design. Later, with her children grown and married, there was time to travel and assist missionaries, on a short-term basis, in England, France, Hungry, Turkey, Mexico and Austria.

Thirty years of family genealogical research combined with hidden diaries uncovered in her Grammy's basement inspired a desire to write *Bayou Roots*. These experiences have resulted in her first published book.

April enjoys living in southern Colorado near her son and his large family that includes six of her 12 grandchildren and 10 great, grandchildren. Her older daughter lives in northern Colorado and a younger daughter and her family live in Orlando, Florida.

Contact: Aprilholthaus@wolfcreekwriters.com

APPENDIX

The Phonemic Dictionary of English—an explanation by Rowena L. Adamson, written in conjunction with her Ph.D at Georgetown University.

This is a systematic readout of phonemic symbols for English, so that, when a sound, or chain of sounds, in the left-hand column makes sense to you, you will be able to find traditional spelling, grammatical identification, and correct meanings of the real word, all three, over in the column at the right side.

Systematic rotation of the phonemes of a language makes it possible to record all of the potential options for combining the two kinds of sounds, "open" and "closed" and for discovering all of the units-of-understanding shared between the speakers of that particular language.

Rowena L. Adamson, Ph.D candidate, Georgetown University

Copyrights of Rowena L. Adamson

Letters

Words

Grammar and Syntax

Style

Philosophy

The Nature of Language. 1982

Other Work

Operetta "Overland with the Pioneers 1951
Rowena Records, two songs for English language study
. . . . 1961
The Street Names of Washington, DC. 1979
The Street Names of New Orleans 1977
Handbook on Rug Hooking 1959
Bookmarks: number and number words prepared for TOEFL students
Metric system explained 1994
Trade Names: Grammar Games, The Grammar Tree, Trustin Print, Edutainment, Linguistic Research Associates

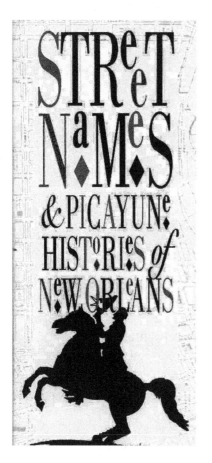

Nocturnal Reflections
Poems and Prose

by
Elaine Rowena LaCoste Adamson

Born in Lafayette, LA
November 15, 1917

BIBLIOGRAPHY

Adamson, Rowena Elaine LaCoste, *Nocturnal Reflections*, 2004.

Arthur, Stanley Clisby, *Old New Orleans – Walking Tours of the French Quarter*, Pelican Publishing Company, Gretna, 1990.

Asbury, Herbert, *The French Quarter: An Informal History of the New Orleans Underworld*, Thunder Mouth Press, 1936.

Barnes, Nancy, Stories to Tell, *An easy guide to self-publishing family history books & memoirs*- publisher, 2010.

Brasseaux, Carl A., *The Founding of New Acadia, Beginnings of Acadian Life 1765 – 1803*, Louisiana State University Press, 1987.

Brasseaux, Carl A., *Acadian to Cajun, Transformation of a People –1803-1877*, University Press of Mississippi, 1992.

Cass, Deborah, *Writing Your Family History – a practical guide*, The Crowood Press, 2004.

Dollarhide, William, *Map Guide to American Migrations 1735-1815*, Heritage Quest, 1997.

Ferrano, Pat, et.al. *Hearts & Hands: The Influence of Women and Quilts on American Society*. San Francisco: Quilt Digest Press, 1987.

Garrett, Elizabeth Donagby. *At Home: The American Family, 1750-1870*, New York: Harry N. Abrams, Inc., Publishers, 1990.

Grossman, Julian. *The Civil War – Battlefields and Campgrounds in the Art of Winslow Homer*. Abradale Press/Harry N. Abrahams Inc., 1991.

Gutkind, Lee. *You Can't Make This Stuff Up*. First Da Capo Press, Perseus Books Group, Philadelphia, PA., 2012

Horridge, Patricia, et.al. *Dating Costumes: A Checklist Method*, Nashville: American Association for State & Local History, 1977.

Illustrated Atlas of the Civil War, Alexandria, Virginia – Time/Life Books, 1998.

Laderman, Gary. *The Sacred Remains: American Attitudes Toward Death, 1799-1883*. New Haven; Yale University Press. 1996.

Martinez, Elsie and LeCorgne, Margaret, *Uptown / Downtown –Growing up in New Orleans*; The Center of Louisiana Studies, The University of Southwestern Louisiana, Lafayette, Louisiana, 1986.

Ouchley, Kelby, "Benjamin Butler." KnowLA Encyclopedia of Louisiana. Ed. David Johnson. Louisiana Endowment for the Humanities, 6 September 2013. Web. 1 June 2016.

Pitot, James, *Observations on the Colony of Louisiana from 1796-1802*, trans. Henry C. Pitot (Baton Rouge: Louisiana State Univ. Press, 1979), p.5.

Sacher, John M. "Civil War Louisiana." KnowLA Encyclopedia of Louisiana. Ed. David Johnson. Louisiana Endowment for the Humanities, 6 June 2011. Web 1 June 2016.

Samuel, Martha Ann Bret Samuel and Ray, The Great Days of the Garden District And the Old city of Lafayette, By the Parents' League of the Louise S. McGehee School, 1961.

Sublette, Ned, *The World That Made New Orleans*. Lawrence Hill Books, Chicago, IL., 2009

Taylor, Joe Gray, *Louisiana, A History*, WW Norton, 1984.

Varhola, Michael J., *Everyday Life During the Civil War: A Guide for Writers' and Students and Historians*. Cincinnati: Writer's Digest Books, 1999.

Vlach, John Michael. *Back of the Big House-The Arch of Plantation Slavery.*

Wilds, John, Dufo, Charles L., Cowen, Walter G., *Louisiana, Yesterday and Today – A Historical Guide to the State*, Louisiana State Press, 1996.

Wilson, Nancy Tregre, *St. Charles Parish: A Brief Look at the Past*, 2010.

Family Letters and Stories 1866 to 2012 —Frances Knight Mandell, Almira LeeAnna Nick Gruner, Rowena Nick Pennock, and Rowena Elaine LaCoste Adamson.

Houma Court House Records Department, Mary Champagne and staff.

-2018-

Bayou Roots, a Louisiana story of family legacy,
published in the tricentennial year celebrating
the founding of New Orleans.

-1718-

Made in the USA
Columbia, SC
09 February 2021